DATE DUE

Group Design and Leadership

GROUP DESIGN AND LEADERSHIP:

Strategies for Creating Successful Common-Theme Groups

Henry B. Andrews
Curtin University of Technology
Perth, Western Australia

Allyn and Bacon
Boston • London • Toronto • Sydney • Tokyo • Singapore

Copyright © 1995 by Allyn and Bacon
A Division of Paramount Publishing
160 Gould Street
Needham Heights, Massachusetts 02194

Library of Congress Cataloging-in-Publication Data

Andrews, Henry B.
    Group design and leadership: strategies for creating successful com-
    mon-theme groups/Henry B. Andrews
        p.   cm.
    Includes bibliographical references and index.
    ISBN 0-205-16197-9
    1. Group psychotherapy. I. Title.
    [DNLM: 1. Psychotherapy, Group. 2. Leadership. WM 430 A5662g
1994]
RC488.A66543 1994
616.89'152—dc20
DNLM/DLC
for Library of Congress   93-49555
                                                      CIP

Printed in the United States of America

10 9 8 7 6 5 4 3 2 1   98 97 96 95 94

CONTENTS

PREFACE

Group therapy has evolved from modest beginnings to become a major treatment method used in a wide variety of settings. Currently, group work shows a clear trend toward more specialized applications. A high percentage of groups qualify as "common-theme" efforts which have a focused problem and a time-limited nature. Common-theme groups address a wide range of problems. For example, focused group therapy is used for stress management, bulimics, parents with problem children, couples, sexually abused children, and the bereaved. Also qualifying as common-theme groups are a significant number of programs which help people cope with almost any medical condition imaginable, such as diabetes, cardiovascular problems, cancer, spinal cord injuries, and multiple sclerosis. Another category of related groups addresses disorders such as phobias, and problems with social anxiety. Also, there are many common-theme groups devoted to helping people alleviate posttraumatic stress disorders resulting from rape, incest, war, and other traumas. There are hundreds of varieties of such groups, and frequently they have similar goals, such as providing members with accurate information, giving support, and assisting in the development of coping techniques.

Increasingly, psychologists and other helping professionals are required to design and lead groups for a targeted population with a specific problem. This book provides suggestions and guidelines appropriate for common-theme groups utilizing processes associated with brief group therapy. The book is organized around the theme of therapeutic factors, which are the elements largely responsible for the positive changes that occur during a group experience. Leadership strategies that promote positive change are reviewed and discussed in detail. Also, circumstances that might create a harmful experience for a group participant are reviewed, and guidelines for a safe and ethical practice are outlined.

This book does not promote any particular theoretical orientation associated with a specific "school" of psychotherapy. There is no convincing evidence that variables which help or hinder the progress of a group are a product of the theoretical orientation of the leader. Despite the complexity of groups, it is possible to develop a model for group practice that is not merely an extension of individual therapy. I hope this book makes a contribution toward such a development.

ACKNOWLEDGMENTS

I would like to thank the following reviewers who read and commented on the manuscript: Diane Derr, The Hamot Institute for Behavioral Health, Erie, Pennsylvania and Catherine Flanagan, Director of Forensic Psychological Services, Seaford, New York. Thank you also to Madalyn Kelly and Pradip for their helpful suggestions and assistance with the manuscript. Most of all I would like to thank Jenny Thornton for her thoughtful suggestions, helpful critical reviews, and most of all for her support and encouragement.

ABOUT THE AUTHOR

Henry B. Andrews (Ed.D., University of Tennessee) lives in Perth, Western Australia. He is currently a Senior Lecturer and Coordinator of the Counselling Psychology program in the School of Psychology at Curtin University of Technology. He was previously an Associate Professor at Wright State University in Dayton, Ohio. He has published in a number of different areas relating to health psychology and rehabilitation psychology.

1

THE EVOLUTION OF COMMON-THEME GROUPS

Group work has evolved from modest beginnings to become a major treatment method used in a wide variety of settings. The scope and variety of group therapy has become increasingly complex, and has compounded the problem of determining what a group is or how people are affected by a group experience. Group therapeutic work has evolved in a social context which has supported professional specialization of all kinds. Therefore, treatment approaches have become more time-limited, focused and diverse. Doubts about the relative value of group and individual approaches have persisted, and controversy about the negative effects of groups continues. Despite the lack of definitive answers to some questions, group work has continued to expand, and a significant portion of the population has participated in a group experience of some type.

BEGINNINGS OF THERAPEUTIC GROUPS

Joseph Pratt was one of the first practitioners who recognized the power of group interventions. In 1905 he began his work with tuberculosis patients, offering support and information on an outpatient basis. Pratt's methodology was simple, not unlike group designs which are still widely used; he would meet once or

1

twice weekly in a group of as many as 30 patients. Each meeting would begin with an optimistic lecture about the characteristics of tuberculosis and the recommended treatment regime. Afterwards, successful patients reinforced the positive nature of the meeting by telling their stories and offering further encouragement (Schaffer & Galinsky, 1974).

Pratt's approach probably represented one of the first examples of the use of the group format to facilitate adjustment and recovery for a homogeneous selection of patients. His effort was an early prototype of many group interventions that are now used for clients with a specific medical diagnosis. Pratt recognized the utility of forming groups composed of people with a common diagnosis. The obvious similarities in the membership facilitated opportunities for gaining information and support. The "common-theme" approach to group design and leadership has exemplified many current group interventions.

A few years after Pratt's initial work L.C. Marsh, a psychiatrist, began to use very similar methods with psychiatric inpatients. Marsh's program was even more formalized. Patients attended classes, took notes, wrote papers and were graded on their assignments. He also conducted groups with all hospital personnel who regularly came into contact with the patients. Marsh emphasized the importance of creating a total therapeutic atmosphere within a treatment setting (Sadock & Kaplan, 1983).

Around the same time, J.L. Moreno introduced his group concepts in the United States. Moreno had been involved in group work in Europe since 1910 and was the originator of psychodrama and many other group techniques. He was one of the first practitioners who attempted to systematically use the curative possibilities inherent in groups. After he came to the United States, Moreno was active in a variety of group efforts. For example, he commonly used expressions such as "encounter," and "sensitivity training," in the 1920s, and began marathon groups in the 1930s. Moreno recognized the powerful influence the group might have for therapeutic purposes. Rather than adapting group work from an existing theory of individual therapy, he tried to develop a theoretical framework unique to groups (Moreno, 1970). Moreno's work still influences current practice, and psychodrama is still almost solely confined to group settings.

Freud's writings also strongly influenced group work before World War II. The publication of *Group Psychology and the Analysis of the Ego* (1922) extended psychoanalytic concepts into a group setting. Freud viewed group work as a recapitulation of the family, with the leader in the role of a parent. Most analysts who became involved in group therapy adopted a similar strategy and transferred a theoretical perspective designed for individual work to a group setting, including analytic group work with children (Smith, 1980). A different perspective was developed by Bion and Durkine (Polcin, 1991) who felt that the leader needed to address the forces produced by the group, instead of focusing solely on the individual, and proposed a group analytic procedure in which the analyst acted as a parent figure.

Other significant forces in group work evolved in England following World War II. Many returning soldiers needed assistance, and some psychiatrists and psychologists became interested in meeting the demands for mental health services by offering group treatment. In addition to the existing Tavistock Clinic, the Northfield Military Hospital project became a center for a variety of new approaches. S.H. Foulkes (considered by many to be the initiator of psychoanalytic group therapy), Wilfred Bion, and Maxwell Jones were influential in the development of group work.

One stream of group development in the United States was associated with Kurt Lewin and the National Training Laboratories (NTL) in 1947. Until Lewin's time, most researchers had focused on the individual as a unit of analysis, but Lewin held a contrary view. He believed that a group had a life and structure that was unique, and therefore, an individual in a group could only be understood in the context of the group dynamics. The NTL was a major contributor to the development of theoretical and practical issues associated with groups, and has continued to be a significant center for the design and practice of group approaches. In addition to personal development activities, NTL has expanded the study of group process to include methodologies for creating organizational change (Johnson, 1988).

Another influential center for group work was developed on the West Coast. In 1962 the Esalen Institute in California was started, and it became an influential growth center. Esalen became famous (or infamous) for its innovative group work. Many prominent group leaders were involved with the Esalen experiment. Fritz Perls practiced his gestalt therapy in groups at Esalen (Perls, 1969), and William Schutz was noted for the "Esalen Eclectic" type of group experience (Schutz, 1967).

There were a number of well-known theorists also noted for their influence on early group work. These therapists included Dreikurs (1957) who further developed Adler's individual psychology, Berne's transactional analysis (1966), and Rogers (1970) for client-centered work. Consistent with many other writers at the time, their group procedures were adapted from dyadic work.

Unfortunately, the tendency to assume that individual therapeutic approaches can be transferred automatically to group work has persisted. Of course, many techniques used with an individual can be applied to a group. Nonetheless, there is not an automatic transfer of theory or practice from dyadic to group settings.

> *This problem may have its origins in the early development of group psychotherapy theories. These theories seem to have their genesis in theories of individual psychotherapy, psychopathology, and personality development . . . The result is that the group discipline has borrowed, and failed to modify, a major portion of its conceptual identity (Kaul & Bednar, 1986, p. 673).*

The consequences of borrowing theory has resulted in a questionable conceptual foundation for some group practices. Many practitioners have assumed that if a particular theoretical perspective worked with an individual then a modified process would be equally effective with a group. A frequent result has been group leaders performing one-to-one interventions in front of a group, and hoping that the other participants will learn by watching, a strategy that produces minimal effects on the observers (Block & Crouch, 1985). This style of leadership prevents the development of the group, and probably inhibits the impact of a number of possible therapeutic factors.

IMPACT OF THE HUMAN POTENTIAL MOVEMENT

The human potential movement during the 1960s and 1970s significantly influenced group practice. Group experiences were often used in an attempt to raise consciousness, to assist in remediating social ills, and for a variety of other reasons. Many people attended black-white encounter groups in an attempt to face, and hopefully resolve, their racial biases. There were T-Groups (training groups) of all types, and "sensitivity" group experiences that ranged from nude encounters to sessions led only by a tape recorder. George Bach became famous for the marathon (12–48 hours) of continuous group meetings, and the Synanon "game" became popular. The Synanon experience often consisted of participants conducting extreme verbal attacks on a chosen individual. Apparently, there was a Synanon belief that being forced to conduct a vigorous defense made one psychologically strong. Many participants have described such groups as an experiential embodiment of Nietzsche's belief that "That which does not kill me makes me stronger."

Unfortunately, many groups were led by people whose only training was a prior group experience. As a result there were many negative incidents reported by participants. Problems with encounter and sensitivity groups eventually led to the American Psychological Association's (1971) development of a code of ethics for conducting growth groups.

Not surprisingly, this period of extensive, and sometimes bizarre, group activity received extensive media coverage. Of more concern, the sensational reports often left a lasting impression in people's minds about what a "group" was. The public perception of a group experience became associated with direct confrontation, brutal honesty, and a "let it all hang out" philosophy (Rowe & Winborn, 1973).

There seems to have been a decline in the personal growth types of groups over the last 20 years. At least there has been a decrease in groups called "personal growth," "encounter," and the like in the literature. The reasons for fewer growth groups are not clear. Encounter groups did not produce the magical changes that were promised or expected (see for example, Lieberman, Yalom, & Miles, 1973). It may be that growth groups still exist, but in a different form, such as in the many varieties of self-help groups. A more likely explanation is that clinicians have found it sensible to construct specialized types of group experiences, rather than trying to manage participants with widely disparate objectives and expectations.

COMMON-THEME GROUPS

The current literature suggests most group designs emphasize a specific problem common to the entire membership. This move toward specialization has been demonstrated by the synthesis between medical treatment and psychosocial services. Increasing acceptance of the biopsychosocial model as a basis for both understanding and treating illness and injury has resulted in the evolution of many diagnosis-specific groups.

> *Generic personal growth experiences and general counseling and psychotherapy groups will be replaced, in part, by short-term, theme centered interventions. This trend toward abbreviated groups is already evident in the expanding literature on specialized groups for both children and adults (Dies 1985, p. 721).*

The use of the term "common-theme" is to distinguish these types of groups from general psychotherapy groups, if such a distinction can be made reliably. In the last 10–15 years an extensive diversity of focused groups has been offered to the public. Examples are groups for bulimics (Stevens & Salisbury, 1984), postmyocardial infarction patients (Stern, Plionis, & Kaslow, 1984), women with premenstrual stress (Levitt, 1986), parents of asthmatic children (Abramson, 1979), pregnant women on methadone (Mackie-Ramos & Rice, 1988), and a support group for widows (Llewelyn & Haslett, 1986).

The previous examples of common-theme groups represent participants who have a homogeneous problem; other groups have a collective focus such as stress management or assertiveness training (Richards, Burlingame, & Fuhriman, 1990). Common-theme groups usually attempt to provide accurate information, encourage discussion and generate mutual support. Other typical objectives are to assist the members to develop short- and long-term coping strategies, and specific skills. The leaders often employ structured exercises, role playing, homework assignments, and a variety of techniques to accomplish their objectives. As part of the process, the leaders focus on collective problems for discussion and help the participants explore troubling thoughts, feelings, and behavior. Also there are attempts to encourage reports of successes and to facilitate interpersonal acceptance and support.

Although the description of a typical common-theme group seems leader directed, an autocratic approach to group process is not suggested. However, leaders do attempt actively to create processes that will aid the members' adjustment, or assist in the remediation of a particular problem. Obviously, a heavy-handed approach to the process of the group will not make use of the members' abilities to help themselves, or each other.

There has been at least one attempt to systematically determine how common-theme groups are constructed. Richards et al., (1990) selected 115 reports on groups with a thematic approach, and the studies were classified on a number of variables. The results indicated that a variety of themes is represented in common-theme groups, including social skills groups (the most frequent), criminal offenders, medical conditions, and depression (second most frequent). Groups varied in size from 3–27 participants, and were considerably diverse in structure. In general, the reports on theme groups suffered from a lack of specificity. Much more information is needed about the groups' composition, which processes are used, and what elements are actually responsible for change in the members.

COMMON-THEME AND GENERAL PSYCHOTHERAPY GROUPS

The qualifier "general" is employed somewhat arbitrarily to distinguish therapy groups that are designed to resolve troublesome patterns of behavior from common-theme groups. Participants in a general therapy group normally focus on behavior that may not have necessarily a common diagnosis or problem. In a general therapy group one person may attempt to work through parental conflicts, another may want to learn how to reduce interpersonal isolation, and a third might want to remove blocks to intimacy with others. Rather than the common-theme groups' emphasis on one primary and specific difficulty (such as, diabetes, agoraphobia, bulimia, or being a survivor of a sexual assault), the general therapy group participant usually has a long-term interpersonal concern. Scheidlinger (1984) has suggested these types of groups should focus on the restoration of serious personality problems and others (Joyce, Azim, & Morin, 1988, p. 5) have described them similarly.

Members are . . . functioning adequately in work and social roles, but complain of dissatisfaction or chronic difficulty

*with relationships. The focus of long-term group therapy is
the resolution of long-standing interpersonal dysfunction and
characterological problems.*

General therapy groups are likely to run for a longer period of
time than common-theme efforts, which tend to be time-limited
and of much shorter duration. One reason for the general group
being relatively longer-term is that often it relies on the development of the interpersonal process, or transference reactions, to
create therapeutic possibilities. An additional difference between
the two types is the member's relative need for information, which
usually is higher in most common-theme groups. The demand for
accurate facts could be acute when a diagnoses is first made,
particularly when the medical condition is life threatening (Stern,
Plionis, & Kaslow, 1984).

COMMON-THEME AND SELF-HELP GROUPS

Since the general aims of common-theme groups are often similar, it is not surprising that the underlying structure of many of
them are comparable. There is also an obvious correspondence
between many self-help and common-theme groups. Most self-
help groups also are composed of members who have a collective
problem or diagnosis. Self-help members also want to receive
helpful information, advice, and support from other participants.
    Although most common-theme groups have comparable ob-
jectives, there are differences. Self-help organizations frequently
espouse an operational philosophy or a "way of being" which is
based on history and tradition and describes how the participant
may improve. For example, new members of Alcoholics Anonymous are quickly exposed to the "12-step process." More experienced alcoholics in recovery instruct new members with the
procedures associated with the 12 steps, and how adherence to the
process will lead to their eventual rehabilitation. Common-theme
group participants may hear some of the same promises when the
professional leaders endorse a particular methodology or theory.
The major difference is that (hopefully) the professional leader
can produce some supporting evidence other than history and
tradition.

Common-theme groups usually have professionally trained leaders, while self-help groups are often led by nonpaid volunteers who are recruited after they have completed the initial treatment program. The ability to move from the role of beneficiary to helper is probably one of the components that makes self-help organizations viable and popular. Additionally, the helpers often discover a sense of personal renewal through the process of assisting others. Leaders of self-help groups presumably receive additional benefits from the feelings of altruism that result from nonpaid activities (Silverman, 1986).

Common-theme groups typically exist with the same members for a specified period, which allows group cohesiveness to develop over time. In contrast, self-help groups often vary in composition from one meeting to another. Consequently, the group "life" is limited to one meeting. While the open membership of self-help groups allows easy access for potential members, the constantly changing membership makes it difficult to develop highly cohesive groups.

Self-help organizations are less likely to use formal psychotherapeutic techniques, or train members in specific psychotherapeutic skills. Their operating methodology usually emphasizes positive support and enhancement of existing strengths, rather than psychological growth through insight and confrontation. By contrast, common-theme designs often include competence training for its members, and promote a particular theoretical orientation.

One final, but significant difference between common-theme and self-help groups is the frequency of program evaluation. Common-theme groups are much more likely to have their effectiveness evaluated, at least anecdotally. There have been very few controlled studies that have evaluated the effectiveness of self-help groups (Gartner & Reissman, 1984). There is evidence that self-help groups have provided a social support function that reduces psychological stress (see for example, Schaefer, Coyne, & Lazarus, 1981). Another study (Galanter, 1988) showed some positive effects for former psychiatric patients who regularly participated in structured Recovery Inc. groups. The Recovery Inc. program used peer-led groups as a primary treatment modality, but also stressed the importance of continuing professional care. After participating in the program, the members showed lower levels of distress and higher levels of employment than non-participants. The positive gains by the members were attributed to two factors: first, there was intense social cohesiveness created among the members; second, the members learned a structured cognitive process which helped them cope more adaptively with stress.

Nonetheless, there have been some concerns raised about self-help groups. It does not appear that the outcomes of such groups are always positive. Lieberman and Gourash-Bliwise (1982) evaluated peer-led and professionally conducted self-enhancement groups for the elderly. The peer-led groups showed an increase in the psychiatric symptomology of their members while those who had participated in professionally led groups showed a decrease in symptoms. Groups with professional leaders also produced an increase in self-esteem by their members. A related study (Lieberman, 1990) found that an evaluation of 36 self-help groups for new mothers reported higher levels of distress and problems than existed in an equivalent random sample.

Another criticism of self-help groups is that they are attended disproportionately by white women from the higher socioeconomic classes. There has been evidence that the needs of men, minority groups, and the lower classes have not been addressed by most existing self-help groups, at least in the United States (Taylor, Falke, Shoptaw, & Lichtman, 1986).

Although questions about the effectiveness of self-help groups are unanswered, there are a few conclusions that have importance. First, the precepts that apply to common-theme groups are markedly different from self-help groups. Determining the relative efficacy of self-help groups is more difficult because a successful outcome in a peer-led group may be defined quite differently from success in a professionally led group. Second, there is currently no *conclusive* evidence that self-help groups produce effects markedly different from therapy groups. Third, despite the studies which demonstrated undesirable outcomes from self-help efforts, the negative effects of professionally led groups have also been a source of concern (Dies & Teleska, 1985). Finally, it is likely that self-help groups will become more legitimized, and this will mean more professional influence on how they are conducted. This will probably lead to a concomitant increase in the blending of therapy and self-help group designs (Jacobs & Goodman, 1989).

BRIEF THERAPY AND
COMMON-THEME GROUPS

Another trend that has paralleled the movement toward common-theme groups is the increasing use of brief therapy approaches. A review by Toseland and Siporin (1986) found that about two-thirds of all group studies published between 1965 and 1985 reported a duration of less than 20 sessions, which suggests that most group therapy qualifies as time-limited. Even a cursory survey of the current literature gives the same impression.

Budman (1981) outlined some advantages for limited group therapy, including the contention that clients are confronted with the issue of responsibility for change much more in the brief format. Similarly, Klein (1985) suggested very specific functions for short-term groups that are consistent with the aims of common-theme approaches. Good selection and preparation of the participants is a primary goal, as is the development of realistic treatment goals for the time available. Furthermore, the group interaction should emphasize a mobilization of resources and stress ego functioning. Patients are also encouraged to take active responsibility for promoting their own welfare. In the brief model, the leader emphasizes the client's strengths and models appropriate behavior. Often leaders may use cognitive and didactic strategies to enhance learning. Perhaps most important, most brief groups are designed to emphasize a clear process that is obvious to the participant.

> In the first stage one talks about matters that are usually kept private. In the second stage, one tries to arrive at decisions about how to handle these previously private issues, and third, one takes action on those decisions (Klein, 1985, p. 325).

Straightforward, active and concentrated forms of group treatment have been endorsed by many of the researchers associated with brief groups. However, there is a major difference between groups that are merely short-term in length, and groups that employ clear brief therapy strategies. Fuhriman and Burlingame (1990) reviewed 22 examples of groups where there was "conceptually planned short-term treatment . . ." (p. 94). The review discovered considerable inconsistency with a number of variables, but agreement on several factors, as follows.

Initial Structure

Some leaders thought how members are selected and the composition of the group was essential, while other reports ignored or minimized selection and composition issues. Thirteen of the groups allowed new members to enter after the group began, while nine groups remained intact for the life of the group.

Group size varied from 4–10 members. Almost all leaders excluded people with serious pathology, with the exception of groups designed solely for inpatient settings. Nearly all the reports stressed the need for a pre-group orientation, which was accomplished usually by an interview process, although some used structured group experiences.

The planned length for most of the groups was less than 20 sessions, although a few examples were open-ended. Except for inpatients, most groups met weekly. The length of the sessions varied between one and two hours, but most met for 90 minutes.

Process

Without exception, all the reports underscored the requirement for a good working alliance between the leader and each member. Nearly all the reports emphasized the necessity for common objectives, and for the objectives to relate clearly to the process. There was also a need to develop a homogeneous view of the purpose and direction of the group early in the process. Members were prepared, kept aware of the time limitations, and focused on the objectives of the group. Similarly, Piper (1991) suggested that the essential requirements of brief group therapy include a membership with similar problems, constant focusing on common issues, and using the time-limited nature of the group to advantage. That is, the therapist makes the limitations of the group part of the process, so that participants are clear about what can be achieved in the time available.

It appears that brief therapy approaches share many commonalities with common-theme groups. In fact, most brief therapy efforts seem to require a focus on a common problem in order to be effective within preset time limitations. There is consistency within the methodologies of both types of groups and it would appear that the general objectives of each are compatible.

EFFECTIVENESS OF COMMON-THEME GROUPS

There is no body of literature that specifically addresses the universal effectiveness of common-theme groups. Common-theme groups illustrate an almost infinite variety of focus and structure. The outcome assessments also vary considerably and many of them are anecdotal. There are numerous case studies that have reported the effectiveness of common-theme groups with almost any problem one could imagine. One attempt to review theme-oriented groups assessed 115 studies between 1980–1988 (Richards & Burlingame, 1990). They found large variations in size, structure and number of sessions, but reached no conclusions about their overall impact. The lack of clear conceptual models and attention to therapeutic factors were cited as serious deficiencies. Common-theme research reports have tended to rely on anecdotal data to support their effectiveness. Controlled studies are rare, and estimates of their effectiveness are difficult to make.

Views on the relative efficacy of group work as a whole vary considerably. One extreme position has been taken by Corsini (1988, p. 34)) who claimed that "... I know of absolutely no really good research at all in group therapy." He does however, feel that group therapy is effective as viewed by the experiences of his clients. A more optimistic view is reported by Kaul and Bednar (1986). They have completed a series of reviews on group literature over the last 40 years and have concluded that groups are in the main, effective. Although many reports are methodologically flawed, there are also a vast number of clinical reports that attest to the effectiveness of group approaches with many different kinds of problems.

Regardless, the specific circumstances associated with success, such as length of treatment, type of therapy, and characteristics of leaders and clients, remain unidentified for the vast majority of groups (Kaul & Bednar, 1986). The lack of knowledge about the specific conditions associated with successful outcomes is undesirable, but understandable. Given the complexity inherent in group work, it is not surprising that research has proven so difficult. Despite a shortage of evidence that could suggest that specific processes will result in predictable outcomes, psychologists (and other professionals and paraprofessionals) continue to lead groups.

INDIVIDUAL VERSUS GROUP THERAPY

As the previous discussion indicated, groups have been shown to be an effective way to treat many types of problems. Another practical question is how group approaches compare with individual therapy. An extensive review of the literature by Toseland and Siporin (1986) concluded that group therapy is as effective as individual work, and may be more effective at times. Tillitski (1990) reviewed their work and performed a meta-analysis of nine studies that met essential criteria for experimental comparisons. That is, the investigations used pretest-posttest designs and compared group, individual, and control treatments. In total, there were 75 measures and 349 subjects. The meta-analysis showed that the positive effects for group and individual treatment were equivalent, and superior to no treatment for adults. With children, individual approaches were more effective than groups, and the converse was true for adolescents.

When compared with individual work, it appears that groups produce an equivalent and substantial therapeutic effect. Nevertheless, as is true of many studies about therapy, the positive effects may only be viewed generally. The question of what kind of group would be effective with a given individual was not considered, and the data needed to provide an answer does not exist at present.

It is helpful also to estimate the relative merits and limitations associated with group and individual therapy. Lakin (1985) argued that there are substantial differences between what group and individual therapy can provide. Compared with dyadic work, some of the major advantages of groups include:

1. There is the opportunity for multidirectional peer support, rather than unidirectional professional support. People can learn to give support and guidance, as well as receive it.

2. Participants have more opportunities for taking direct action and trying different behavior. Patterns of behavior with a variety of people can be observed, and new behavioral alternatives can be structured. Modeling and observational learning opportunities are also significantly increased in groups.

3. In contrast to dyadic therapy, the therapist in a group is not the final arbitrator of reality. Sources of feedback are considerably broadened by including other group members' perceptions and suggestions.

4. In a group, nonproductive therapist-client relationships have a better chance of being avoided, or altered if they do occur. In an exclusively dyadic relationship unhelpful patterns of interaction can be maintained more easily. While unhelpful transference and countertransference relationships cannot be circumvented completely, coleaders or group members often can mediate a troublesome therapist-client relationship.

5. An additional possibility is that an individual can have more opportunities to develop autonomy in a group situation. In a properly led group an individual is required to function independently, and dependent relationships can often be observed and modified.

Of course, there are disadvantages for group work compared with dyadic therapy. There is less time focused on any person and the intrapsychic material cannot be analyzed extensively. The group does not represent a normal social situation, therefore generalization from the sessions to the person's life may be more difficult—although the same criticism could be true for individual counseling.

If the group situation is designed and led properly, there are many advantages to working in groups as opposed to dyads. It is not necessary however, to create an either–or situation. Dyadic and group therapy have distinct advantages that may be used, dependent on the needs of the client. A clinician is faced with the usual problem of trying to make a proper assessment about which therapeutic modality might be most appropriate for a particular individual.

2

PREGROUP DESIGN AND PLANNING

Planning a group requires attention to many factors. Leaders need to consider variables such as the learning objectives, the size of the group, its composition, and what process is used to select members. Other important considerations involve how to advertise the group, and what type of pregroup training might be appropriate and effective. The intake interview is particularly important, and much of the early work of the group can be enhanced significantly if the first contact with potential members is well planned and conducted.

GROUP DESIGN PROCESS

The following procedure is a suggested outline for the group design procedure that covers initial planning through to postgroup evaluation.

Pregroup Design

1. Determine the major reasons for offering the group.
2. Set the general objectives for the group.
3. Determine the probable group size and composition.
4. Advertise the group.
5. Complete an intake/screening process.

6.   Set the objectives for the group and a general strategy for the meetings.

7.   Develop a procedure for the ongoing and final evaluation of the group.

8.   Develop a specific plan for the first session.

Continuing Group Design

9.   Plan the process of the group session by session with particular attention to:

   a.   personal and interpersonal issues.
   b.   potential impact of the therapeutic factors.
   c.   leader behaviors appropriate to the current dynamics of the group.

10.   Develop transition mechanisms and procedures that will aid the individuals after the group has ended.

11.   Plan and implement a postgroup evaluation.

REASONS FOR ORGANIZING GROUPS

We assume that the major reason for developing a group is to provide services to clients. This assumption might be true at times, but in reality groups are often started because of the personal or professional needs of the leader. In some cases organizational demands cause groups to be created. Occasionally groups are formed in response to requests from potential clients. The reason for the group's formation is not a trivial matter and may influence the actual process far more than anticipated. A simple illustration of how "origins influence process" is provided by comparing three contrasting groups that are all targeted toward the same population.

Assume Group A is designed primarily so the leader can fulfill a requirement for a higher degree. Groups that attempt to provide a service to people *and* meet academic requirements are particularly vulnerable to external influences. For example, the educational institution may have size or composition requirements that seriously affect the selection process. Additionally, there may be specific requirements for how the group is to be evaluated that impinge on the structure and process. If the academic supervisor favors a particular theoretical orientation, the student leader may tend to conduct the group consistent with the supervisor's bias. In all these situations it is not unusual to find the academic pressures altering the selection of participants, leadership style, or method of evaluation. Of course the academic influences need not necessarily be negative, but in Group A there is the potential for the client's welfare to be secondary to the leader's need to meet a class requirement.

In the second example Group B was started because the leader was told by his supervisor to develop groups to alleviate high caseload demands. Such a goal essentially means that some clients who might have preferred individual therapy may now be pressured to participate in groups instead. The pressure to serve more clients could result in participation by people who are not suited for groups. Compromising selection criteria obviously increases the possibilities of members having negative effects from the experience. At the very least, Group B may contain people who are more at risk for an unhelpful experience.

Group C was developed by a private practitioner who wants to increase practice income. Unless extra care is exercised, the clinician could easily allow the client's welfare to become secondary. Monetary pressures could increase the tendency to accept applicants who are not suited for group work. Accepting a questionable referral to please a colleague would also be a temptation. While Group C is in progress, if a participant becomes discouraged and wants to leave the group, the leader might pressure the individual to remain in the group in order to meet financial goals.

Even if Groups A, B, and C were directed to address the same type of problem and contained similar types of clients, the motivation and style of the leader, and the group design and process will probably differ markedly. Therefore, one of the first decisions the leader must make concerns, "Who is to be the primary beneficiary of the group?" More specifically, is the group being formed *primarily* to meet academic requirements, reduce organizational pressures, make money, or for other reasons? Obviously, groups often are conducted for other than purely altruistic purposes. Being clear about why the group exists allows the leaders to keep that reason clearly present in the planning process, and during the group. Ethical practice requires that the client be protected from harm and the task becomes much more difficult unless the forces and constraints connected with the development of the group are part of the process.

A related concern is the probability that organizational demands might influence the group while it is in progress. One early proponent of group work (Berne, 1966) warned of the hazards involved in balancing the needs of the leader with those of the organization sponsoring the group. For example, the management of the organization may have originally agreed that the client's welfare came first, but that is no guarantee that a sudden shortage of staff or money might not threaten the agreement later. The obvious course is for potential leaders to think carefully about, and plan for, possible client and organizational conflicts of needs before their occurrence. Whatever the motivations or constraints associated with the group, they need to be kept as an obvious part of the continuing group design.

Setting General Objectives

Once the leaders have clarified why they want to start a group, more specific planning is possible. Strategies used with brief group interventions provide constructive guidelines for designing groups. Focused planning strategies involve clarifying what is to be accomplished, identifying member behaviors associated with the stated objectives, and structuring an appropriate therapeutic process to produce the desired changes (Dies, 1983b).

Properly set outcome objectives makes the entire design process much easier to accomplish. A useful place to begin a group is to give some thought to major objectives under categories of "attitudes," "knowledge," and "skills." In other words, at the end of this group:

- What attitudes will the members have toward the problem?
- What specific knowledge will they have about the problem?
- What skills will the participants gain by the end of the group?

The relative number, type, and specificity of the objectives may vary considerably, dependent on the theoretical orientation of the leader, or the type of group planned. It is easier to write specific objectives for a stress management group than it is for a group that will address existential issues. However, in both situations there is still a need to think about outcomes before the group begins.

The leader of either group needs to have some general goals in mind in order to begin planning. Of most importance is that the leader knows what is to be accomplished, and can discuss desirable outcomes with potential members during the intake process. Applicants may suggest (directly or indirectly) new objectives to the leader during the interview. Initial objectives may be modified after the leader reflects on the final composition of the group.

GROUP SIZE

After the leaders have some idea of the objectives for a group, the next step is to decide how many, and what types of participants, would be appropriate. Discussions about group size are common in the literature, but there is little empirical data that guides the practitioner when trying to determine the proper group size.

In attempting to form a group, leaders encounter the usual problem of balancing multiple interacting factors. Group size is dependent on the type of group, its objectives, the time available, and skills of the leader. Conversely, the size of the group partially dictates objectives, the time needed, and the types of skills needed by the leader. Despite the complexities, leaders have to start somewhere, and the size of the group will be dictated mostly by its purpose.

One helpful way to determine group size is to consider how much the group will attempt to formally educate the members, as opposed to an emphasis on using the interpersonal relationships for learning. Decisions about how much guidance may be necessary, or how extensively the members' interactions will be used for learning will dictate, at least partially, the size of the group. Groups which primarily seek to educate participants can obviously accommodate larger numbers. As the group moves toward more general therapy a corresponding reduction in size is advisable. A smaller group is necessary because processing the interpersonal actions will require more time, and a larger number of people naturally means there are more relationships to process.

Another major factor that influences group size is the comfort level and personal style of the leader. Some leaders are comfortable with groups of 12–15 members, and others feel that groups from six to eight members are ideal. Generally, leaders that emphasize learning through interpersonal actions would tend to have smaller groups. Group size is a matter of preference rather than fact. There are many reports of successful therapy groups ranging from as few as four participants to as many as 20 members. The ideal recommended size is from 6–10 participants.

Until research demonstrates otherwise, determination of the group size remains one of both comfort and safety. Particularly when a leader is inexperienced and working alone, the smaller group probably is preferable. Negative effects are more likely in larger groups because of the difficulty the leader has in making accurate assessments about how each person is being affected by the interaction.

LENGTH OF MEETINGS

Similar to other group practices, there is no conclusive research to guide how long a group should meet. Most leaders choose 1–2 hours per week, but there are many time variations reported in the literature. For unknown reasons, the most frequently chosen length of a group appears to be 1.5 hours per week. The reason for this length probably has to do more with tradition than anything else. Since there are no clear relationships between group size, the length of a meeting, and positive outcomes, how long a group meeting is becomes a somewhat arbitrary decision. The meeting period is probably based on such variables as convenience for the leader, scheduling constraints, or a rough estimate of what needs to be accomplished.

In practice, considering the time needed to plan and critique the weekly sessions, a total time commitment of about double the weekly length of a group is needed normally. This time requirement would be the same for a coleadership situation, or a single leader who plans alone and spends some time with a supervisor. The actual time spent in supervision will be dependent on the prior experience of the leader. The 1:1 ratio has proved to be a reasonable estimate of the leader's time commitment unless the group is unusually large, or the format requires an extended group model, such as a full-day meeting.

GROUP COMPOSITION

At this step in the pregroup planning, the leader will want to get an idea of what type of people would be appropriate for the planned group. Once she or he is clear about the membership, the next step is planning how to advertise the group.

Some careful thinking will be necessary to accomplish this task. Membership considerations include some ideas about what personal characteristics and level of functioning are needed to use the group successfully. Some basic considerations include attention to variables such as gender, age, and types of problems.

For instance, a person appropriate for a stress management group would have current identified stress symptoms, and inadequate stress management techniques. The group would probably be appropriate for both men and women. Adults within a wide age range would be appropriate due to the universality of stress problems. As is true of any successful group participant, a reasonable level of intelligence and verbal ability would be desirable.

In contrast, the proposed functional characteristics of a general therapy group member would be more difficult to specify. Along with normal verbal and intellectual abilities, the person needs to be able to work successfully (for example, give and receive feedback) in a group. Both men and women can be included, and a wider range of interpersonal problems could be addressed. A heterogeneous composition would be more likely to foster natural conflict and interaction among members, and these combinations can be productively illuminated by the leaders. Unfortunately, ". . . what factors should be similar and what ones should be different remains empirically unanswered" (Fuhriman & Burlingame, 1990, p. 16). A detailed meta-analysis that related composition, structure, and duration of treatment concluded that composition was most important when the group was long-term and unstructured. Unfortunately, exactly what type of composition was related to structure and duration was unknown (Waltman & Zimpfer, 1988).

An issue many theorists consider important is whether groups should have a common problem focus. In the previous examples the consensus of the literature has been followed. The little research that is available has suggested that groups composed of people with varying problems, such as in the general therapy illustration, provide more opportunity for interpersonal learning. On the negative side such groups tend to start to work more slowly, have more trouble with factors of acceptance and universality, and more attrition. By contrast, common-theme groups have more opportunities for cohesiveness and intergroup support, and provide a rapid problem focus while probably having fewer initial opportunities for learning from interpersonal actions (Klein, 1985).

Initial ideas about composition have to be flexible because the ideal membership may not eventuate after the group has been advertised or recruited. The importance of considering composition is that it forces the leaders to think clearly about the type of person who is most appropriate for the planned group. Setting objectives has created a framework to use during the intake interview. The objectives can be discussed with potential members, and they can be evaluated by reference to the proposed model.

A noticeable omission from this discussion has been a consideration of how to select members to balance the interaction in the group. If there were an unending supply of potential members and sufficient time to interview them all, and some reliable way to predict precisely how they will function in a group setting, then balancing a group might be possible. A sufficient supply of clients, and the time to interview them all rarely exists. Even if there were a large supply of potential group members, most leaders would have difficulty predicting the prospective member's interpersonal behavior in the group. Rather than attempting to engineer the composition, it would be much more profitable to spend the equivalent time and energy with good intake interviews. People who are ready to profit from a group experience can then be selected, rather than the leader trying to form some hypothetical balancing function.

OPEN VERSUS CLOSED GROUPS

One final determination in initial planning is whether the group is to be open or closed. This means, does the initially selected group continue for a specified period or will new members be added as old ones leave? The hypothetical stress management group probably would be a closed group for the duration because it would tend to have a structured and progressive focus. Participants would be taken through a program of education and skill training. Although general therapy groups often begin closed they will add members infrequently when there is an opening. There is no definitive research on which model might be best. It would appear, as the examples illustrate, that the nature of the group largely prescribes the open or closed philosophy.

ADVERTISING THE GROUP

Now that the preliminary planning for the group has been accomplished, the next step is advertising. The leaders will either select their own clients, or indicate to other professionals that the group is being planned and what type of person would be a likely referral. When one's own clients are involved, it may be relatively easy for the therapist to decide which clients are appropriate for the group, but communicating that criteria to other professionals may be more difficult. Referrals could be invited by providing a description of the types of appropriate problems, and level of functioning expected from a potential member. The problem characteristics and functional requirements can be developed into a brief format to be sent to colleagues. Other details, such as session times and length of the group, could also be included as appropriate and necessary. Further particulars of the estimated size of the group, its composition, and appropriate age range can be listed. Where and how the groups are advertised is largely a function of the leader's knowledge of the local community, but there are a few guidelines that might be helpful if there is a need for active recruitment of clients.

As the frequency of specialty common-theme groups increases, there may be a need for professionals to recruit potential members. Practitioners in public agencies also may want to attempt better matching of clients with available services. Wilson et al. (1987) suggested some strategies for the marketing of group services. When ethically appropriate, issues such as product, promotion, place, and price are worthwhile recruiting devices and can be used successfully to solicit members. They used applicable concepts from social marketing theory to successfully recruit members for groups. Two major components of social marketing involve: (1) careful analysis of the intended target audience, and (2) designing the recruitment so what the consumers want or need is adequately addressed. Various strategies were recommended, including focusing on the benefits and opportunities offered by the prospective group. Strategies were oriented to gain the attention of the intended audience when they are not distracted by other events. They suggested recruiting individually or in groups where a focused presentation can be made, instead of depending on a brochure to gain peoples' attention secondary to another activity. The authors also emphasized the need for personal contact with people so they have an immediate opportunity to join the group. Consideration of the physical, psychological, and monetary costs of participation was also important. Their strategies were successful in recruiting participants who did not initially respond to the usual approach of sending out announcements of the group and hoping enough acceptable people replied.

Summary of Initial Planning

- Consider motivations and constraints influencing the group.
- Determine the general type of group.
- Consider time requirements for leadership and supervision.
- Set objectives for the group.
- Decide size, composition, and member characteristics.
- Advertise briefly and specifically to the target population.

INTAKE INTERVIEWS

Good intake interviews are essential, and can positively affect the actual process of the group after it begins. Many clinicians can testify to the problems that can be created in a group when the leader has not completed the pregroup preparation properly. The lack of a good intake interview not only risks a real mismatch of expectation in the group, but increases the probability of both attrition and casualties. There is substantial agreement among researchers that the potential for casualties can be greatly reduced by a careful screening process, and that the majority of psychological injuries are a result of inadequate screening (Anderson, 1985; Dies & Teleska, 1985; Hartley, Roback, & Abramowitz, 1976). The American Psychological Association requires that a potential client be informed about treatment procedures (Principles 4.01 and 4.02). In particular, therapists are to discuss ". . . the nature and anticipated course of therapy." (Principle 4.01). The Association for Specialists in Group Work (ASGW, 1989) requires a screening interview and informed consent. One major reason for the initial interview is so the leader and member have congruent aims for the experience. Additionally, the screening process can identify a member who is unlikely to benefit by the group experience. Weiner (1983a, p. 319) has asserted:

> *Every patient referred by a colleague must be evaluated individually for his fit with the group therapist and the group currently available. Regardless of the descriptive diagnosis, the patient must be evaluated in terms of his interaction with the group—an evaluation that cannot be performed by the referring person or agency.*

Conducting intake interviews is not only well worth the time involved, but can enhance the progress of the group (Shapiro, 1978). There is no question that there will be more of an opportunity for positive gain when everyone knows what is expected, the structure is clear, and people are relatively homogeneous in their expectations. Although there are many specifics associated with intake interviews, there are at least four major tasks to be accomplished:

1. Reconcile any differences between the leader's and applicant's objectives.
2. Evaluate the applicant's suitability.
3. Begin to form a working alliance with the member.
4. Conduct specific preparation for the group work.

Although each of the four factors will be considered separately, the interview situation usually involves a substantial integration of all four. The following discussion will assume that the person has been referred to the group and the intake interview is the first meeting between the prospective member and the leader. If the person is previously known to the interviewer, the procedures can be easily modified.

The process begins with a brief explanation of why the interview needs to take place and the objectives of the meeting. The potential members need to know that the primary purpose of the interview is to consider whether or not the group is suitable for them. If this introduction is handled clearly and sensitively then the leader creates a situation where the individual can be accepted or screened from the group without seriously involving the person's self-esteem. Interviews need not become pass-fail predicaments, more a process of examining matching expectations and capabilities. It is helpful if the interviewer is aware of other appropriate community referral resources. If some applicants do not choose to enter the group, they can be readily referred to an appropriate resource.

The first task, and perhaps the key issue in the screening interview, is to determine if what the person wants from the group will actually occur. Often people have very unrealistic or distorted ideas about what happens in groups and the actual impact of the experience. Such ideas will need to be addressed during the interview. In general, however, what the leader will want to accomplish is a reconciliation between the expectation of the member and the leader. If all the group members and the leader are not headed in the same direction, valuable group time may be spent processing (overtly or covertly) the dynamics of the mismatch in expectations. The importance of the intake interview cannot be stressed too much. Although the intake process will add to time expenditure, the net gains in safe and effective groups are considerable.

After initial statements about the purpose of the interview, the next agenda is usually a consideration of what the applicant hopes to gain from the group experience. Normally, asking about why the person is interested in coming to the group will provide the necessary opening to pursue the questions of the person's present functioning and expectations. This opening allows for a determination of the specific nature of the person's problem and whether the group can provide the kind of assistance that will be helpful. In contrast, if the interviewer begins the interview stating a lot of details about what the group will do, there is the risk that the demand characteristics of the situation will influence what the potential members will say. Applicants may then be tempted to modify their treatment goals to accommodate the anticipated group design.

Potential leaders must take responsibility for understanding how potential clients are functioning, and the kind of experiences they need to help them. Personal or organizational needs to fill a group cannot be allowed to override the proper evaluation of the applicant's suitability. Of course, there will be very few situations where the applicant's and leader's expectations will fit exactly. Despite the lack of a perfect match of expectations, there needs to be a clear and honest discussion of differences. There is no reason to increase the possibility that the person might be pressured to fit the group profile, and thus risk a negative outcome. The leader must insure that ". . . expectations members have for the group are realistic, clarified, and mutual" (Anderson, 1985, p. 269).

Other practitioners have constructed more thorough ways of determining whether the person will adapt well to the group. Budman and Gurman (1988) have expressed concern about use of an interview only for group selection. They feel that a dyadic process is often a poor predictor of how the person will behave in a group setting. The writers devised a procedure where the potential member is introduced to the group, participates in a small group exercise, and then is involved with the entire group. Following the experience clients decide whether they want to continue participation or not.

Once the leader obtains a reasonably clear idea about what the person wants, there can then be a discussion about what is planned for the group. The initial objectives can be used effectively during this process. Differences between the plans and applicant's hopes need to be explicitly explored and reconciled. There may be some differences between the leader's plans and the person's needs at the end of the interview. Such an occurrence does not preclude the person's participation. The important point is that applicants know exactly where they stand in relation to the group. After the initial exploration, the leader may not feel the person is suitable for the group. In such cases, there is enough information available to indicate clearly why the person is not suitable, and for the leader to suggest an alternative referral.

One example of both mismatched expectations and inadequate screening involved a clinician at a community mental health center who advertised a group for women with weight control problems. The potential leader was very experienced in working with overweight women and had worked out a reasonable design. However, no screening of consequence was performed, and nine women were accepted for the group after telephone call inquiries. During the first meeting the leader discovered she had eight overweight women about 25–40 and one mildly anorexic 21-year-old as members. In this case the leader handled the situation without undue harm, but more subtle mismatches are very commonly missed. It is alarming how many groups are formed and conducted after respondents answer an advertisement. The applicants then enter a group without any type of preliminary evaluation.

Apart from a gross mismatch of needs, the most obvious reason to decide whether people will fit into the planned program is that they may be unsuitable for reasons related to basic personal style or psychopathology. Most group leaders suggest that people who are extremely withdrawn, anxious, or antisocial are obvious examples of individuals unsuited to most group work. Brandes (1977) reported on two adolescents who were inappropriate for groups. One person was 19 years old and was too anxious to function well which resulted in negative effects for him and other group members. In another case, a homosexual female (18 years old) was too angry and provocative for the group to handle and needed more individual work before being placed in a group. In both cases, intake interviews may have prevented the mismatches.

Finn and Shakir (1990) have offered helpful information about placing borderline patients in groups. They noted the borderline person's tendency to perceive people or situations in black or white terms. Such behavior often invites scapegoating from other members. Potentially damaging situations can be avoided by careful selection, and/or by referrals for individual therapy until the person is more interpersonally functional.

A recent study (McCallum & Piper, 1990) used a measure of psychological-mindedness to predict dropouts from brief psychoanalytic group therapy. The assessment demonstrated that 62% of the lower scoring clients left the groups early, but only 2% of those high on psychological-mindedness left prematurely.

Unfortunately, there are few examples of these types of helpful clinical reports available and leaders have to learn by trial and error what people are unsuited for group work. There is certainly little agreement about who should, or should not, be included in group treatment (Unger, 1989). Despite the lack of clear evidence to guide selection, leaders need to attempt to exclude people who appear to be at risk. People with serious and refractory pathology often can experience a pressure to change in a group setting. When they fail to accomplish the hoped for changes, their resulting reactions can create more anxiety, depression, anger, or other negative effects in both themselves and others (Parker, 1972).

The obvious unsuitable group candidate may not be a problem for screening; difficult clients may not always present with such obvious deficits in functioning. Since the leader will have some idea of the basic design of the group prior to the interview, the relative importance of significant therapeutic factors can be examined, and the person may be assessed with that in mind. For example, consideration of the person and the curative elements of acceptance and self-disclosure will provide useful screening information.

The most important factor to consider is acceptance. Accordingly, when considering a person for admission, the leader must be able to answer two questions in the affirmative. First, "Will this person be able to participate positively in the process?" Second, "Can I *actively* accept this person during the group?" Or stated another way, "Will the group and I be able to accept and support this person?" Accurately answering both questions is largely a function of training and experience, although on the latter question, Naar (1982) has recommended that only those people with whom the leader feels comfortable be allowed in the group.

Other writers also have stressed the importance of the leader-member relationship (Murphy & Cannon, 1986; Thayer, 1986). The leaders must carefully examine their reactions to the interviewee and anticipate how they and the other members might be able to relate to the person on a long-term basis. Due to excessive demand for services, or other pressures, sometimes there is a temptation to override a sense of discomfort about a person's suitability. Regardless of the pressures, placing an unsuitable person in a group is problematic.

The types of self-disclosure the person divulges in the interview often provide clues about the individual's readiness for group work. If the applicant spontaneously discloses much potentially sensitive material not related to the reason for the group, it may be a warning to be careful about admitting the individual. The person may need to work through other concerns prior to being ready for group work. For example, an applicant for a stress management group spent most of the intake interview discussing the (sad) state of his marriage, which was the primary source of stress. He was referred for marital work rather than accepted for the group.

In a common-theme group, a question such as—"Other than the problem focus of this group, are there any other concerns that you have that you might want help with?"—may elicit some idea of whether the potential member is likely to need to deal with other significant issues that could be inappropriate during the group.

If the person is suitable for the group, the interview can progress naturally to some of the basic preparation for the group experience. Ground rules, fees, structure, and some description of the process can be addressed. However, the most important task to be accomplished is to begin the formation of a reasonable working relationship with the potential member. Forming an initial working alliance is an essential part of the entire interview, and involves the prerequisite skills of communicating empathy and acceptance to the participant.

In short-term groups the process of contracting with the participant is recommended. Contracting would be a helpful idea for any type of group, and there are several items that could be part of the initial contract. Most important is a delineation of the goals of treatment and the treatment approach that will be used to address the identified problems. If the client has been referred to the group, the contracting discussion also can be an ideal time to communicate the referral information and to obtain a clear commitment from the person about group attendance (Klein, 1985).

PRETRAINING FOR GROUPS

During the intake, the leader can attempt to prepare the member for later work using therapeutic factors that have been helpful in producing positive change. Statements such as, "I think you will find there will be several people in the group who have similar experiences," foreshadow the development of group cohesion and universality. Helping behavior can be promoted by statements like, "One of the most important functions of the group is for the members to help each other." The interview ideally can end with the distribution of some resource materials to the client. The new participant might be asked to do some background reading, complete baseline charts, keep a diary, or other tasks. There is no risk in trying to both prepare the person for the group and involving the new participant in productive work before the first meeting. Asking the person to complete assigned tasks before the group begins also emphasizes the idea that each member will be asked to take responsibility for preparation and involvement.

In addition to the more informal group preparation previously discussed, a number of leaders have attempted to pretrain people to operate effectively in groups. These studies have utilized audiotapes and videotapes, interviews, role induction techniques, and a variety of methods. In one example Piper (1991, p. 422) suggested that ". . . the notion that brief therapy requires only brief preparation is likely false." In his work with clients who had suffered a recent loss, both the referring person and the program interviewer were involved in verbal and written preparations. He felt that a repetitious preparation was more effective with people who had recently suffered an upsetting event. Similarly, Budman and Gurman (1988) strongly endorsed the need for group pretraining, particularly in short-term groups.

Numerous studies have supported the efficacy of pregroup training, although many of the reports have been confounded. (Kaul & Bednar, 1986; LaTorre, 1977). A recent review (Piper & Perrault, 1989) found few studies which were methodologically sound and concluded that the research evidence to support the efficacy of pregroup training was not conclusive. One problem was that the vast majority of the pretraining efforts reported lasted less than a total of one hour. Such a short period of induction would have little chance of preparing one for the complexity of group work. One area where there were significant effects was in pretraining increasing attendance and preventing dropouts. Since people who terminate from a group prematurely are higher risks for negative effects, some pregroup preparation might be justified based on that finding alone.

Although a particular procedure may not meet all the rules for a precise research design, anything that clarifies the role expectations for participants is helpful. Power (1985) has suggested that the potential members could participate in a preparatory group as part of the selection process. This participation not only assists accurate screening but prepares the person for the experience. Nonetheless, a preparatory group is, of course, a real group and carries all the normal risks and benefits for the participant. Its major advantage is the leader can observe the person in a group situation and the applicant can sample the experience prior to making a commitment. From both perspectives, the process seems to have much to offer. The negative possibilities include the obvious: A person who has a bad experience in a trial group will require very effective postgroup management by the leaders. Where the groups' membership is open, the trial procedure is worth experimentation.

Gauron and Rawlings (1975) outlined a comprehensive procedure for group pretraining. Potential members were provided with guidelines, ground rules for participation, suggestions for the feedback process, and a goal-setting schedule. Finally, prospective members viewed a videotape of the group they were to join. The authors felt that these procedures both helped the new person integrate into the group and facilitated the treatment. They also felt an additional benefit was that the induction procedure forced the leaders to articulate their treatment process.

From a clinical perspective, the ideal preparation would probably involve an actual videotape of a group demonstrating desirable patterns of interaction. Following the viewing, there is a brief interview where the prospective members' reactions and concerns are discussed. Where groups of a similar nature are in progress, such a procedure might be possible. Most leaders will probably have to use less sophisticated and time-consuming types of preparation. Brief guidelines for group participation, ground rules, and some type of assigned preparatory activity to be completed prior to the first session is considered minimum preparation for a new group member.

PREPARING FOR
PREMATURE TERMINATION

One final concern for the leader is to brief the potential member on the procedures to be followed in case the person decides to leave the group before its scheduled completion. First, it needs to be made clear that the decision to leave is respected and that neither the leader nor the group pressure the person to change the decision. Second, the member could be encouraged to discuss with the group the reasons for leaving. At least a phone contact with the leader is an alternative if nothing else is possible. The leader needs to ensure that the person who is leaving has adequate support. If warranted, a referral for additional treatment might be proper as well. The procedure for premature termination can be included in the general guidelines for the group and can be stated again during the first session.

Summary of Intake Interview Concerns

- Matching of expectations
- Assessment of applicant's potential functioning in the group
- Evaluation of potential for acceptance by leader and group
- Contracting on treatment goals
- Preparation for the group

SETTING SPECIFIC OBJECTIVES

The final design of the group and initial objectives can now begin. Each group member's needs can be considered relevant to the initial objectives, and revisions may be accomplished as necessary. Objectives that reflect the major knowledge, skills, and attitudes that will be the focus for the experience can be reconsidered and modified. This brief list can become the foundation for the actual work and periodic evaluation of the group.

For most common-theme groups, the next step in the design process is a tentative session-by-session outline of topics or procedures that are to receive major emphasis. In some cases, it is helpful to estimate how much time is needed for each activity. The exact sequence of themes, activities, or exercises can only be approximated. Once the group begins, the participants may have some different ideas about how the group needs to proceed.

3

HOW GROUPS WORK

This chapter considers many of the reasons why groups are an effective way of offering therapy to people. The discussion begins with an overview of group dynamics. Next, the therapeutic factors, which seem to be the core ingredients associated with positive change, will be discussed in detail. Finally, the literature on stages of groups is considered as it relates to the process of group development and individual change.

GROUP DYNAMICS: WHY DO GROUPS WORK?

The term "group dynamics" refers to the intrinsic nature of groups, the ways in which the group and its individual members affect each other, and the relationship of this interaction to issues of group development, structure and goals (Munich & Astrachan, 1983; p. 15).

As frequently used, the phrase "group dynamics" can refer to almost anything that happens in a group whether it is understood or not. The definition is certainly broad enough to cover almost everything that might happen in a group, yet not specific enough to offer much guidance about what actually makes a group work. The vague nature of the definition is not due to any theoretical or semantic deficiency of its authors, but reflects the inherent complexity of groups. However, the definition does include some useful concepts.

Taking the statement's last point first—a group has some structure and goals which may be related. At least the members and leaders have some individual goals which may be compatible. In any case, the beginning point for considering group dynamics usually involves a consideration of the general objectives. One way of approaching the situation is to consider two contrasting groups, the T-group and a highly structured group.

In the classic T-group the leader frequently offers no structure at all, but simply sits down and waits for things to happen. As a result of no formal input from the leader, there was subsequently a structure developed by the group, which then went through a normal process of development with minimal interference from the leader. By contrast, the T-group might be compared with another group where the leader actively directs the situation. The goals are precisely defined and the group interaction is structured in an attempt to accomplish preplanned objectives. Deviations from the design are minimal. In this latter case the group probably can have more difficulty going through the normal phases of development because of the structure. However, the same group *forces* are present regardless of the tight structure. Both groups can be shaped partially by strong developmental forces that exist regardless of the relative degree of control exercised on the group. Developmental forces in the T-group are more predominant and probably more subtle in the highly structured experience.

So far three major variables involved in the consideration of group dynamics have been mentioned. First, there are the stated goals; second, the degree of structure imposed by the leaders; and third, how much the group is encouraged, or allowed, to pursue its normal developmental sequence. A fourth variable, which is also of considerable importance, is the coleaders' relationship (if the group has two leaders). The quality and quantity of their interaction will substantially affect the group.

A fifth significant factor is a consideration of the leader's or leaders' relationship with each member of the group. The final (and sixth) component of importance is the members' relationships with each other. The interpersonal relationships are not only numerous, their quality often dictates what is called the "group mood."

If these six factors could be analyzed and their effects clearly separated, the task of understanding group dynamics would not be so difficult. Of course, the problem is that all the variables listed so far, interact with each other. For example, the degree of structure affects the developmental process, which affects all of the relationships, which affects the group goals, and so forth. Adding to the difficulty of analysis or prediction is the fact that the reciprocal influences often occur at once. Therefore, a hypothetical seventh variable is the complex interactions of all the six previous components, plus other factors which have not been mentioned. The net result is a synergistic effect. The complex interactions of variables create a group effect which may be labelled in a variety of ways, often referred to as the group's level of "cohesion." A listing of the variables which have been discussed so far include:

1. Group goals
2. Degree of structure
3. Developmental processes
4. Leader-leader relationship
5. Leader(s)-member relationships
6. Member-member relationships
7. Synergistic effects

It is important to reiterate that all of the factors listed above *will* affect the group regardless of the design. It does not matter whether the group in question is a T-group or a very controlled assertive training program, there will be an influence by the listed elements. Encompassed within some of the above variables are some not-so-obvious factors which may significantly influence the group.

1. Group goals: There are explicit goals which may be congruent for the leader and members, for example, reduction of stress. There are also implicit goals which are often never discussed openly in the group, but are still very much part of the interaction. For example, the leaders may want to have their skills admired; some members may want to develop a close friendship in the

group; and others may want to be completely cured of all their problems. Such "hidden agendas" can radically affect the process in the group, yet they rarely surface to become part of the overt group agenda.

2.   Degree of structure: The term "structure" is used here in its broadest sense. The leader can choose to exercise rigorous control of the process or let the group develop as it will. How much leaders encourage the group to get to know each other, allow negative exchanges to develop and be processed, or encourage interpersonal feedback are examples of the expression of structure.

3.   Leaders' relationships: The quality of the interactions between the coleaders can have enormous influence on the group. Suppose that the two leaders are subtly competitive, seductive, or antagonistic towards each other—to name a few of the possibilities. Almost invariably, members understand and react to the implicit qualitative nature of the interpersonal relationship between the leaders. If the leaders illustrate a relationship incongruent with the stated norms for the group, the impact can be deleterious. On the other hand, if the leaders model what they expect of the participants, considerable gain can result.

4.   Leader-member and member-member relationships: Age, sex, physical size, religious beliefs, ethnicity, personality style, family of origin, and many other variables influence how people experience each other, and consequently, modify the quality and quantity of the interactions in the group. Of most importance is the understanding that *each person has a relationship with each other person and each relationship affects the group in some way.* The initial purpose of the group largely dictates how much the leader might encourage the participants to spend time working on interpersonal relationships. For instance, the leader-member and member-member interactions and relationships can be a major focus in the T-group, but probably receive little attention in the standard assertiveness training group.

Consider also that the overall length of the group, the duration of the meetings, the time it meets, the physical setting for the meetings, and the attitudes of significant others who are not in the group can also influence the quality, quantity, and structure of the interactions. The problem of clearly understanding anything at all about cause-effect relationships in group dynamics probably has become obvious. Groups are complex types of organizations which may be guided somewhat, but are difficult to control, and understanding what makes them work is difficult. There has been some progress toward identifying broad sets of factors which seem to be primarily responsible for positive change in groups. Research on therapeutic factors offer some hope for designing more effective groups.

THERAPEUTIC FACTORS

There appears to be increasing recognition that research with therapeutic factors has considerable potential to provide useful guidance for the group leader. There have been several attempts to identify precisely the components in groups which are responsible for positive changes in group participants. A relatively complete history of the various attempts at classifications of the group curative elements has been outlined by Bloch and Crouch (1985) in their extensive review of the literature. With particular reference to Corsini and Rosenberg (1955) and Yalom (1970; 1975), they identified commonalities in the various systems and produced a list of therapeutic factors which are largely representative of the major efforts to explain why group experiences help individuals to change. Bloch and Crouch described therapeutic factors as distinct elements that are part of the ongoing group and that have powerful effects on the participants. Accordingly, therapeutic factors might be defined as, "An element of group therapy that contributes to improvement in a patient's condition and is a function of the actions of the group therapist, the other group members, and the patient himself (p. 4)."

As the definition implies, therapeutic factors are complex phenomena which might arise from a multiplicity of interactions. For example, a skilled leader may exhibit behaviors designed to increase the level of cohesion in the group, yet whether the overall level of cohesion actually increases predominantly is a result of the subsequent interactions between the group members, as well as the ongoing relationships with the leader. In other words, the actions of the leader account for only a portion of the influence associated with cohesion, and nothing the leader does can guarantee that a group will respond as though there were a simple cause and effect set of circumstances.

Yalom (1985, p. x–xi) has offered a slightly different formulation which parallels the preceding definition. He considers almost all types of groups previously discussed (such as encounter, self-help, psychotherapy) as forms of "therapy" so his definition must be viewed very broadly. In writing about the essential elements which effect change in group therapy, Yalom indicated:

> The front consists of the trappings, the form, the techniques, the specialized language, and the aura surrounding each of the schools of therapy; the core consists of those aspects of the experience that are intrinsic to the therapeutic process— that is, the bareboned mechanisms of change.
>
> Disregard the "front," consider only the actual mechanisms of effecting change in the patient, and we will find that these mechanisms of change are limited in number and markedly similar across groups.

Corsini (1988, p. 15) has adopted a similar position with his contention that, "These mechanisms are considered universal and apply not only to groups run by Adlerians, but to all therapeutic groups."

All these definitions refer to influences which are relatively consistent across groups regardless of theoretical differences reflected by the leaders. These factors act on the members in specific ways and offer potential for positive change. Although the previous explanations refer to therapy groups, the constructs are relevant to common-theme groups. The objectives for common-theme groups are identical. All groups attempt to produce positive change in the participant, and the mechanisms of change are available because of the inherent nature of the group experience. The primary difference in the relationship of therapeutic factors to therapy groups and common-theme groups is probably one of emphasis. For example, many common-theme groups require more emphasis on providing information (one of the identified therapeutic factors), particularly when the participants are newly diagnosed with a "problem." A general psychotherapy group is more likely to use interpersonal interactions for learning, which is another therapeutic component. The emphasis on different curative factors varies with the type of group. The impact, or relative importance of a factor can only be considered in the context of a distinctive group.

The definitions of therapeutic factors which follow generally are consistent with those suggested by Bloch & Crouch (1985). Their definitions are useful for three reasons. First, they have attempted to be reasonably specific about describing the factors. Second, the factors in their classification are a result of careful consideration of the major theoretical formulations and research by Yalom (1975), Corsini and Rosenberg (1955), and a number of other authors. Their consensus description of ten factors contains a reasonably strong empirical rationale, rather than arising solely from their own clinical experience. Third, they have attempted to separate *therapeutic factors* from *techniques* and *conditions for change*. The muddling of the three processes often has been a source of great confusion in group literature. For example, a leader may decide to give a member feedback (technique) because there is a sufficient level of support and acceptance in the group (condition for change). As a result of the feedback the person experiences insight (a therapeutic factor). It is the self-understanding which leads to the positive change even though it may have been preceded by a good technique under optimal conditions. Thus, *a therapeutic factor generally refers to a potential for positive change as a result of the client's response, no matter whether that perception is based on a feeling, insight, new behavior, or the behavior of someone else in the group.*

Despite the interdependence among techniques, conditions for change, and therapeutic factors, the distinction is important. Whether or not the technique is dazzling and the circumstances are ideal, it is the participant's response which is ultimately crucial.

Definitions of the Therapeutic Factors

The following descriptions of each factor should be considered individually and phenomenologically. In other words, the presence or absence of the various components can be determined only by each individual undergoing the experience. The reference point is the perception of each group member. Whereas some factors seem to have an obvious positive relationship with change, the relative impact and ideal balance between the factors will be considered later. Where available, clarifying descriptions and/or examples are cited from research with general psychotherapy or common-theme groups. The ten factors to be discussed are:

1. Acceptance
2. Universality
3. Self-disclosure
4. Insight
5. Learning from Interpersonal Actions (LIA)
6. Catharsis
7. Guidance
8. Vicarious Learning
9. Altruism
10. Hope

Acceptance (Cohesiveness)

This component relates to the individual's feelings of belonging, reciprocal friendliness, and interpersonal valuing. Being understood, accepted and supported is very important, and crucial in cases where the client has revealed something which may be perceived as unacceptable or shameful.

Many theorists and leaders refer to the sense of belonging or acceptance as cohesion. However, the concept of cohesion has been noted for its vagueness and variable meanings (Kaul & Bednar, 1986). Bloch and Crouch (1985, p. 101) have taken a position which places major emphasis on support as a critical part of the idea of acceptance. Their version of acceptance would include a person ". . . not merely being tolerated by his peers and the therapist but also actively *encouraged* [italics added] by them."

The addition of support to this construct is important, particularly in light of findings regarding the value of support in self-help groups. The actions involved in conveying the message "I accept who you are" is different qualitatively from acting in ways which communicate the understanding "I assist and promote who you are." Assisting and promoting another is a much more active process, and usually leads to enhanced feelings of personal acceptance. A group whose members are actively helping and encouraging each other is viewed by both leaders and members as highly cohesive. One attempt to quantify cohesiveness among the members found that intermember levels of empathy, acceptance, self-disclosure, and trust were all significantly correlated. Trust, however, appeared to be an essential constituent of the other components, and may have been the essential component in all of them (Roark & Sharah, 1989).

Acceptance needs to be considered relative to relationships with both the leader and the other members in the group. Ideally, acceptance should be attained by each member and the leaders. With consideration to both positive impact and the avoidance of negative influences on participants, this factor appears to be the most important of the ten which will be considered. There seems to be almost complete agreement among all practitioners and researchers that this component is extremely important to all types of therapeutic groups (see for example, Lieberman et al., 1973: Lakin, 1985), and the vast majority of leaders agree with Cartwright's (1968) contention that a "sense of belongingness" is essential for a group participant in order for the group to be used effectively. Whether the group is oriented toward psychotherapy, support, or a specific concern, intergroup acceptance is a primary issue. Positive change may occur without support and acceptance, but it is a lot easier to accomplish when such elements exist.

Additional research has shown further support for acceptance as crucial in single-session groups of female oncology patients (Arnowitz, Brunswick, & Kaplan, 1983). The component was listed prominently in inpatient brief therapy (Marcovitz & Smith, 1983), and in brief dynamic therapy of 10–20 sessions (Poey, 1985). Similar results were also reported by brief group work with bulimics (Robinson-Smith, 1985).

Universality
One of the major feelings clients report is that they feel isolated with a problem. For example, individuals often report feeling that "No one has ever felt this bad or thought such horrible things." Universality arises when the group participant realizes that other members have comparable thoughts or experiences, usually felt as a sense of relief from psychological isolation and that understanding contributes to improvement.

As previously discussed with reference to self-help groups, one of the major curative forces is the realization that "We're all in the same boat." A typical example is Drob and Bernards' (1986) research with genital herpes patients. Participants felt that the major benefit from their group experience was an alleviation of the loneliness and isolation produced by the disease. Similarly, Lieberman (1983) found that universality was the most highly rated therapeutic factor in eight different types of self-help organizations, despite the fact that all of them had different goals, norms and belief systems. Duhatschek-Krause (1989) found that along with increased feelings of hope, groups for the seriously ill and their families reported universality as a major cause of positive change. Such feelings are commonly reported in all types of groups, particularly when stigma might be attached to the diagnosis or identified problem. Common-theme groups naturally lend themselves to the development of feelings of universality, because their very reason for existing in the first place is related to a problem that all participants share.

Ideas of universality may occur in situations other than those associated with a specific problem or diagnosis. Members often report that knowing that their responses have been similar to others can bring relief. Members of a 36-week general therapy group felt that feelings of universality were the primary reason for change (Koch, 1983). Children of divorce, in a short term group, also rated universality as the most important component creating change (Lesowitz, Kalter, Pickar, Chethik, & Schaefer, 1987).

Specific circumstances might vary, but "feeling crazy," being depressed, anxious, or being in severe emotional pain related to some life events is not unusual. Developing an understanding that the intense feelings are shared is often very therapeutic. For instance, Llewelyn & Haslett (1987) found the experience of universality was instrumental in producing beneficial responses by widows in a support group.

The feelings may seem too intense or "bad" to be normal at the time. Later the person discovers that many others have felt exactly the same way and this fact alone often reduces the loneliness that such negative self-judgments can produce. It is likely that many of the positive effects from groups reside solely in the reduction of feelings of loneliness that result from feeling that one's experiences or reactions are unique.

Self-Disclosure
At its most basic level this factor simply involves "The act of revealing personal information to the group (Bloch & Crouch, 1985, p. 128)." Obviously this definition implies that what is self-

disclosed has some significant implications for the discloser. The revelation might involve extremes of experience, such as detailing a painful history of being sexually abused or expressing mild annoyance to another group member. The act of self-disclosure can be judged only on the basis of its meaning to the discloser. What a person feels is self-disclosure *is* self-disclosure. It is not the facts of the situation which determine the impact of the revelation, but the affect which is associated with the information. Obviously, the leader will have to carefully evaluate the sensitivity of any new information that a member offers the group.

There have been few studies of the actual effects of member self-disclosure. Client self-disclosures have shown to be related to higher levels of cohesion, interpersonal liking, and reciprocity (Stockton & Morran, 1982). It also appears that the level of intimacy reflected in the content of a discloser is related to the level of acceptance previously displayed by the interpersonal transactions (Kirshner, Dies, & Brown, 1978). Research about self-disclosure has been difficult due to definitional problems. Objectively determining what is and is not a self-disclosure has not been an easy task. As the definition implies, only the discloser can verify whether he or she disclosed personal information.

It seems that acceptance and self-disclosure have a reciprocal relationship, and it is hard to imagine that meaningful self-disclosures are not strongly related to feelings of acceptance in most group situations. It seems reasonable that self-disclosure is often used to gain feelings of acceptance. The disclosure is in some way communicating that "I have the same problems you have," or, "I have suffered like you." This commonality of experience or feeling was evident in a report of the importance of self-disclosure in a parents' group (Hausman, 1979).

Common-theme groups probably elicit a high level of self-disclosures, particularly when the disclosures are related to the problem focus of the group. For example, one of the major ways Alcoholics Anonymous members strive for change (or to maintain change) is through extensive revelations about their past. In effective groups it is likely that most of the self-disclosures are related to the groups' reason for being (*the* problem), rather than reflecting a broader range of concerns. Self-disclosures which address issues clearly not related to the reasons for the group's existence are probably not conducive to overall cohesion. If, for example, a group which was created for the purpose of assertiveness training began to have extensive discussions about the members' marital problems, it is likely that some participants may become quite dissatisfied with the process.

Self-Understanding (Insight)

This factor involves several different types of self-understanding. Simply learning ". . . something important about himself" (Bloch & Crouch, 1985; p. 29) is the most inclusive definition. The insight may involve how a person is perceived in the group, or reflect a new understanding about the etiology, nature, or maintenance of the identified problem. Self-understanding has been endorsed as a key ingredient for both dyadic and group therapies. Whether the nature or frequency of insight differs in group settings has not been determined (Fuhriman & Burlingame, 1990).

Self-understanding is similar in some ways to self-disclosure. What is new or important learning can be determined only by the person involved. Of course this therapeutic factor will often be theory-specific, particularly if the insight arises as a result of a dialogue with the leader. Naturally, insights offered by the therapist often reflect her or his theoretical orientation, and could be couched in language associated with behavioral, existential, Adlerian, or a variety of other systems.

Some theorists might argue differently, but what seems to be important about insight is that the person believes the understanding, rather than "it" being a theoretical truth. In other words, many therapists have found that people not only believe very strange things which lead to problems, but they believe equally bizarre explanations which often lead to cures. If an explanation is offered with conviction and the person is ready to receive the new idea, there is a reasonable chance of "insight" occurring. Jerome Frank (1981, p. 20) indicated that a vital part of the healing process was the provision of "a rationale, conceptual scheme, or myth that provides a plausible explanation of the patient's symptoms and prescribes a ritual or procedure for resolving them." Whether psychologists want to refer to any of their theoretical systems as "myths," or agree with the idea that they "prescribe rituals" is another matter. For many clients it may not matter how empirically plausible the explanation is.

The nature of the insight could involve feedback about how other group members see the person, or could pertain to obtaining a clearer or more comprehensive understanding of the nature of the problem; or the person may have gained some new ideas about the etiology of problem behaviors, or the psychodynamics associated with the problem. The person may become suddenly aware that there are positive resources of courage, strength, or caring. In whatever case, there is a new perspective on the self that creates a more positive opportunity for change, or perhaps increases hope for change in the future.

Many group studies have supported the importance of insight in producing change. Self-understanding was rated as one of the most important factors in groups with adult incest victims (Bonney, Randall, & Cleveland, 1986), and bulimic adults (Stevens & Salisbury, 1984). Patients following a myocardial infarction reported that learning how they contributed to their cardiovascular problems was essential in causing change (Stern, et al., 1984). Outpatient psychiatric patients (Kapur, Miller, & Mitchell, 1988) and psychodrama groups (Kellerman, 1985) also found experiences of insight were essential in creating positive change.

Learning from Interpersonal Action (LIA)

One of the major features of groups is their potential to provide opportunities to obtain feedback on current behavior and try out new ways of interacting. LIA occurs when the person either initiates or responds in a new and more positive way in the group. Although LIA may be a consequence of insight, it can be a singular influence, or produce an insight itself. The new behavior can be tested and may be adopted, modified, or abandoned, depending on the results of the new actions. An individual may try being assertive, more supportive, humorous, or affectionate. Group settings provide opportunities for feedback not normally available to the person. It seems important that the new behavior is linked cognitively. The new actions need to be placed in some framework which will guide, and promote the same behavior outside the group.

As was true of insight, the actual structure of the learning from interpersonal actions is likely to be related to the theoretical orientation of the leader. A gestalt group probably would produce different patterns of behavior and cognitive structures than a psychodrama or a psychoanalytic group. Exactly how LIA is promoted or explained, may not be so important as the fact that the person tried something new and more interpersonally effective.

Interpersonal learning has been given prominence by many group leaders. Yalom (1985) emphasized the corrective recapitulation of the family group, as well as the learning of new socializing techniques as eventual consequences of the member interactions. Harman (1988), a gestalt therapist, listed individual awareness and contact as primary goals and also stressed the learning potential inherent in the participant's interactions. Johnson's (1988) work with T-groups highlighted the interpersonal process and the learning that might result as the primary reasons for the groups' existence.

Most literature has stressed the importance of LIA to general therapy groups. The actual learning potential from member interactions may be more limited in common-theme groups, probably because of the strong emphasis on acceptance and universality which might discourage a high level of interpersonal feedback. The research does not support this contention. Learning from interpersonal actions was found to be one of the three most important factors in groups with an outpatient psychiatric population (Butler & Fuhriman, 1983), with inpatients and outpatients (Colijn, et al., 1991; Lesca, Yalom, & Norden, 1985; Weiner, 1983), in a long-term therapy group for depressed people (Llewelyn & Haslett, 1986) with maximum security offenders in a long-term group (MacDevitt & Sanislow, 1987) and in brief (10–20 sessions) dynamic therapy (Poey, 1985). Also, LIA was considered to be the second most important factor in two common-theme groups reported by Llewelyn & Haslett (1986). One group was a widows' support group and the other a group for asthmatics. As is true with other therapeutic factors, the relative emphasis on LIA partially depends on the design of the group, and how the group actually responds is difficult to predict.

Catharsis

Catharsis involves two components. The first is some type of affective release. Second, as a consequence of the emotional expression, there is some feeling of relief (Bloch & Crouch 1985). When catharsis occurs there is no requirement for a particular type of response from the group. The members do not need to show acceptance in response to the release. Catharsis could occur in the process of a self-disclosure, such as when a person reports a previous episode of abuse. If the group supports the person's expression of feelings, then three therapeutic factors can be involved. However, for catharsis to have occurred, just the two components are required, that is, emotional release coupled with some feelings of relief.

Among others, Corey and Corey (1987) have questioned whether catharsis alone can produce much change. They recommended that the leader ensure that cognitive meaning is added to the experience. They felt that the person must label their intense emotions and attempt to understand them before the experience can promote change.

Yalom (1985) viewed the cathartic process differently, and described it as the expression of strong affect which is unique to the person. Following the cathartic expression, the feared catastrophe did not occur. He felt that catharsis was often followed by reality testing. As a result of this process the person may have gained some knowledge of the source of their prior fear of a disaster, and subsequent avoidance.

A careful examination of the differences outlined above produces a process that really involves three stages; there is, first, the emotional expression; second, the relief felt as a result of the expression; third, there needs to be a cognitive framework in which to place the experience. This formulation actually involves two therapeutic factors. The first two stages refer to catharsis, which needs to be linked with an insight, LIA, or an increased sense of hope.

Cathartic experiences normally are spontaneous and functionally related to the group atmosphere. For instance, such experiences naturally occur in common-theme groups, usually contingent on some other therapeutic factors, namely acceptance and universality. Catharsis frequently happens in conjunction with self-disclosure, but not necessarily. The definition of self-disclosure requires the revelation of personal information. Yet catharsis could develop without any information being provided, as in a situation where a member identifies strongly with an event in the group and becomes very sad and cries. All of the reactions could be internally mediated and the person may not provide any explanation for their reaction.

It seems that cathartic experiences are more important in psychotherapy or encounter situations than in common-theme groups. However, a career counseling group for adolescents found it to be one of the most important factors responsible for change. In this study (Kivlighan, Johnsen, & Fretz, 1987) catharsis was defined as:

> *I was able to express feelings very fully; I was able to say what I felt rather than holding it in; I was able to express negative and/or positive feelings about myself, careers and other people.*

Schiedlinger (1984) found that in many adolescent groups catharsis was highly rated for producing change. By contrast, three different studies with outpatients, inpatients, or both populations, found cathartic experiences to be the most highly rated therapeutic factor (Colijn et al., 1991; Butler & Fuhriman, 1983; and Marcovitz & Smith, 1983).

Guidance

Two operations are involved with the therapeutic factor of guidance. First, providing information about a particular condition, diagnosis, or circumstance is considered a guidance function. For instance, guidance may involve providing facts about proper diet and exercise regimes to newly diagnosed diabetics. Second, giving advice or suggestions also would be classified as guidance. Guidance can be implied in situations where a group member might say to another, "It seems that you aren't going to resolve anything until you talk to your wife."

In situations where information or advice is offered, the therapist or group member is trying directly to influence the receiver. Certainly, the guidance function provides new possibilities for knowledge, behavior, thinking, or feeling. In many common-theme groups, particularly where health issues are involved, the provision of both information and coping suggestions can be extremely helpful, and perhaps primary for most of the members. For example, Stern, et al. (1984) reported that in a group for postmyocardial infarction patients, members' need for information was so acute that the group process was being continually interrupted with questions. They subsequently modified the design of the group so that the information giving operations were handled in the initial group sessions. Carefully responding to the members' need for accurate information early in the process allowed other important factors in the group to develop later. Similarly (Llewelyn & Haslett, 1986) reported that guidance was the most important factor in a group for asthmatics. Another study (Andrews, 1991) found that guidance was the most important rated factor in ten short-term "personal development" groups.

How much the guidance factor is emphasized is related to the overall objectives for the group. In psychotherapy groups for example, there appears to be little value in providing information (Bloch & Crouch, 1985), and the offering of direct advice has been discouraged in other types of groups. Nevertheless, providing accurate and current information, or advice, can be an essential part of many common-theme groups, particularly when they are people with a newly diagnosed problem. How much and what type of information might be useful depends on the initial client assessment and design of the group.

Vicarious Learning

This factor is referred to frequently as "spectator therapy" (Corsini, 1988) or "imitative behaviors" (Yalom, 1985). Bloch and Crouch (1985, p. 194) extended the definition to include:

(a) imitation of qualities in others deemed desirable by the observer; and (b) learning that stems from the observer's identification with a fellow patient's specific experience in therapy.

There are many opportunities for imitative behaviors in a group setting, and many therapists have endorsed enthusiastically the idea that the leaders should model the behaviors they want the clients to adopt. Particularly in homogeneous groups, there can be a number of experiences where the member's insight or interactive experience is meaningful to an observer. At least in psychotherapy groups, most studies have shown that vicarious learning alone produces little positive effect in the observers (Bloch & Crouch, 1985). In fact there appears to be a complete absence of any research support for the efficacy of vicarious learning.

Although the little research on the effects of vicarious learning has not been supportive, there is at least a logical case for proposing that a common-theme group might present different opportunities for learning than does a routine therapy group.

First, the organization of a common-theme group would probably enhance the opportunities for identification. The rest of the group, including the leader in many cases, share the same diagnosis or problem, and probably share many similar experiences. Second, because of the similarity in the group, there seems to be increased chances for imitation of those members who have made successful adjustments. Third, due to the structure built into some skill-based common-theme groups, observational learning is inherent in the process. Demonstrating appropriate behaviors has been extensively and successfully used in a variety of therapeutic settings. Regardless, there is an essential difference between most examples of modeling and vicarious learning. In modeling, the trainer deliberately instructs a person in a skill, or a sequence of behaviors. With vicarious learning, there is felt to be a process of spontaneous identification, or imitation, of another's actions.

Altruism

As the definition of "altruism" implies, this factor operates through the member-to-member helping process. Any extension of help to another member, such as support, mutual sharing, or advising can provide positive benefits to the helper. The client experiences the satisfaction of giving something to another—being helpful. It may not be important that people actually be helpful, but only that they *feel* helpful.

Common-theme groups provide abundant opportunities for the altruistic encounter. The natural process of learning to accept and support others, developing feelings of universality, and offering information or suggestions (guidance) provides chances for members to be helpful to each other.

A number of studies have indicated that group participants' altruistic experiences were primarily responsible for significant changes in them. Acute psychiatric inpatients rated altruism and universality as the two most important factors (Whalen & Mushet, 1986), and an inpatient group felt altruistic acts to be the primary influential factor (Kapur, et al., 1988). An epilepsy self-help group (Droge, Arnston, & Norton, 1986) felt altruism was the most important change component, and outpatient alcoholics rated it very highly (Kanas & Barr, 1982). The variety of groups who stressed the significance of altruism suggests that opportunities to help others are probably a function of the climate of the group, rather than being related to the problem focus.

Hope

A successful group fosters the belief that one can get better or feel relief. Frank (1981) has hypothesized that just the expectation of receiving help can be a therapeutic force. Through the group experience, the person begins to see the possibility of resolving, or living with the problems. As Corey and Corey (1987, p. 185) stated:

> Hope is the belief that change is possible—that one is not a victim of the past and that new decisions can be made. It is therapeutic in itself, for it gives members confidence that they have the power to choose to be different. In the group . . . they may encounter others who have struggled and found ways to assume effective control over their lives . . . being associated with such people can inspire a new sense of optimism.

For many people increased hope may arise from the shift from an external to an internal locus of control. Just the realization that one *can* change often leads directly to an increase in feelings of hope.

Whereas the creation of hope is important for any type of therapy, it has been shown to be critical in a number of settings. Groups with relatively serious problems have listed hope as one of the most important factors; pregnant women on methadone (Mackie-Ramos & Rice, 1988), a support group for seriously ill patients and their families (Duhatsckek-Krause, 1989), and alcoholics (Kanas & Barr, 1982). By comparison, both verbal and music therapy groups (Goldberg, McNeil, & Binder, 1988) and personal development groups (Andrews, 1991) ranked hope as the second most influential component.

The homogeneity of common-theme groups may lend additional possibilities for the creation of hope. One of the major reported positive factors in many types of treatment for chemical dependency is the fact that frequently treatment is conducted by those who have been through a difficult experience and have transcended it. Such groups often contain individuals who are advanced in their recovery with drugs or alcohol. They can foster hope in those who are in a beginning phase of treatment. The same dynamics are true for most categories of common-theme groups. For the most part, people would come to problem-focused groups with some feelings of hope for improvement and their optimistic outlook is developed and supported during the experience.

Summary of Research with Therapeutic Factors

In their initial summary Bloch and Crouch (1985) indicated that the overall pattern of research demonstrated evidence of some general patterns of effectiveness for therapeutic factors and types and length of groups. For both long- and short-term outpatient groups, learning from interpersonal actions, insight and self-disclosure were most helpful. With inpatient groups altruism was the factor reported to be most helpful, followed by acceptance and insight. Guidance and vicarious learning were found to be consistently unhelpful for both inpatient and outpatient groups.

Viewed somewhat differently, in short-term groups universality and acceptance were most helpful. In long-term groups insight, LIA and self-disclosure were rated the most highly. In all types of groups vicarious learning and guidance were not helpful. In considering these conclusions, it is important to remember that at times there is difficulty differentiating short- from long-term groups.

Since the original review by Bloch and Crouch (1985), other studies have been located which have attempted to assess participants' perceptions of the value of therapeutic factors. Those studies were mentioned previously within the discussions of each therapeutic factor.

Most of the reported research attempted to use quantitative measures of the curative factors. There are also a few other studies which were primarily clinical in nature. In those cases the authors attempted to explain the curative forces at work in their groups without the support of formal measurement. The clinical studies reported were a representative sample rather than an exhaustive listing, due to the difficulty in locating such reports. Where possible, the author's formulations have been translated into the ten therapeutic factors previously identified.

Few of the groups can be equated on such variables as measurement instruments, type or emphasis of leadership, group composition, and other factors. Therefore, any conclusions drawn from the results must be regarded with great caution.

Nonetheless, there are a few results of note. First, in contrast to the findings for general therapy groups, there is the strong suggestion that guidance activities are a significant factor in a number of situations. First, in groups where a diagnosed physiological condition exists, guidance was rated highly. An asthma group (Llewelyn & Haslett, 1986), herpes group (Drob & Bernard, 1986) and the group for post myocardial infarction patients (Stern et al., 1984) all rated the provision of information or suggestions from others very highly. Second, perhaps surprisingly, one study of psychiatric inpatients also rated guidance of some importance. These results can be directly contrasted with the two bulimic groups where serious physiological problems have been present, but are a result of psychosocial processes. An additional example where guidance was not reported to be helpful was the self-help epilepsy group (Droge et al., 1986). In such cases information about the conditions does not seem to be of much assistance.

Additionally, one study (Andrews, 1991) found that guidance was a highly rated activity for ten groups conducted at a community college which utilized seven different leaders. The groups' objectives were quite heterogeneous, ranging from "self-caring and wellness," to "living with children." The study required the participants to rate the therapeutic factor which was most important for each session at its conclusion. All the other studies reported the members' perceptions retrospectively for the entire group period.

The universal importance of each therapeutic factor is difficult to determine. Poey (1985) offered a list of the relative importance of the curative factors which represented a composite for group leaders using brief dynamic therapy. His views were based on their clinical experience and placed LIA first, acceptance second, catharsis third, and insight fourth. This finding is in contrast with a recent comparative review of brief group therapy by Burlingame and Fuhriman (1990). They found considerable support for catharsis, cohesion, universality, and insight as the therapeutic factors of most importance. Similar findings were reported by Colijn et al. (1991) who reported on 22 Dutch long-term groups of psychiatric in- and outpatients. They found that catharsis, inter-personal learning, and self-understanding were rated as the most important factors.

Relative Importance of the Therapeutic Factors

Reaching any firm conclusions about the relative importance of therapeutic factors is difficult. Due to the variety of measures and procedures used, equivalent comparisons from one group to another are impossible. However, a few tentative conclusions which have implications for leadership seem warranted. First, there seems to be a strong case for attempting to facilitate interpersonal acceptance. Feelings of support are probably necessary before other factors can be effective. It is doubtful, for example, that LIA or self-disclosure can occur frequently in groups which have not reached a minimal level of interpersonal support and acceptance. Although acceptance is therapeutic in its own right, if it is lacking, it would be hard to imagine that conditions for learning are optimal. The other major reason to stress the importance of acceptance is that without the development of cohesion in a group the probability of negative outcomes increases greatly (Dies & Teleska, 1985). At the end of a group the members may not retrospectively rate acceptance as being the most important variable in producing change, yet it may be a prerequisite for the development of many of the other factors.

Universality also seems to be important in many groups. In common-theme and support groups there is inherent homogeneity, and it is likely that this factor is linked with acceptance. Whereas the support and common-theme groups work from the diagnostic premise that "we are all in the same boat", members of general therapy groups may be more likely to view universality as reflecting their commonalities as human beings, even though each person's "problem" may be different.

Self-understanding and LIA were prominently listed over a number of groups, as was catharsis. Certainly LIA is expected to be one of the major curative forces in groups. Conversely, vicarious learning was not prominent in any of the findings. Spectator learning, although an appealing idea, has failed to gain much research support anywhere in this review or in previous literature.

Hope was a significant factor in seven different studies with widely different populations, suggesting that it may operate as an important element in a variety of different types of groups. Of course, hope is an element which is not unique to group settings and it may well be an example of a therapeutic factor that operates strongly in successful dyadic or group endeavors.

Based on the preceding discussion, the following general view of therapeutic factors is suggested. The development of acceptance and universality provides opportunities to increase the level of interpersonal trust or cohesion for the group and productive gain which may be attributed to almost any of the other therapeutic factors, except vicarious learning. Additionally, guidance seems to be emerging as a significant factor in settings where the members have a diagnosed physiological problem.

In many ways the findings from the reviews are not surprising. The most frequently mentioned curative elements occurring in groups are: learning from interpersonal actions, altruism, universality, and acceptance (by leaders and other members). These components are normally unique to group settings.

Perhaps *the* answer is obvious. There are probably a cluster of therapeutic factors which are important in all forms of therapy, such as insight, therapist acceptance, self-disclosure, and catharsis. Other curative elements are unique to a particular type of therapy, whether it be individual, group, marital, or family work.

GROUP DEVELOPMENT

Most group leaders feel that groups progress naturally through developmental stages, and that a particular stage is reflected in the behavior of the participants. In addition, most theorists believe that the stages have common developmental characteristics regardless of the type or specific objectives of the group. Even the one session group has been observed to operate similarly (Block, 1985).

Many conceptual formulations of the stages of groups have been suggested, and many of the differences between the models have been one of emphasis, rather than demonstrating compelling evidence of discrepant processes. For purposes of comparison four models are outlined in the next section.

Models of Group Development

Corey/ Corey (1987)	Yalom (1985)	Mackenzie/ Livesley (1983)	Tuckman (1965)
Initial	Initial	Engagement	Forming
Transition	Conflict	Differentiation	Storming
Working	Cohesiveness	Individuation	Norming
Ending	Termination	Intimacy	Performing
		Mutuality	Adjourning

Even the most casual inspection of the four models reveals considerable overlap in the characterizations of the phases of groups. In particular, Corey and Corey (1987) and Yalom (1985) are almost identical. Other models propose similar developmental processes. Gill and Barry (1982) relate specific leadership behaviors to a three-stage model, which is Formation, Awareness, and Action. Anderson (1985) suggested a developmental scheme based on issues that develop over the life of the group. His TACIT acronym (Trust, Autonomy, Closeness, Interdependence and Termination) described phases of interpersonal concerns shared by the members. His model closely resembled Mackenzie and Livesley's (1983) formulation, which included Engagement, Differentiation, Individuation, Intimacy, and Mutuality. All these theorists agree that groups go through an early period when the group is developing trust and establishing its particular operating style. This forming period requires the members to establish a foundation for future work. The process then moves beyond explicit ground rules and establishes implicit rules about how the group will operate (norming). The ensuing period may produce considerable conflict and anxiety (storming) before productive work (performing) takes place. As this process unfolds, members illustrate the conflict between autonomy and closeness and finally realize that the most worthwhile strategy involves interdependence. In most models, there is the final period of work where the members prepare to close the group and leave each other (adjourning), which can be a highly productive period.

There seems little doubt that most writers believe that groups proceed through a developmental process. However, attempts to empirically confirm patterns of group development have not produced unequivocal supporting evidence. One study (Phipps & Zastowney, 1988) suggested a connection between leadership behavior, group climate, and outcomes for participants. Two general patterns of group development seemed to be evident. One pattern illustrated an "engagement" phase where the members focused on issues of acceptance. The other major pattern resembled "differentiation" where there were higher levels of conflict and an emphasis on differences. In general, the engagement pattern produced better outcomes for its participants. Although these two different patterns produced contrasting outcomes, they did not demonstrate a developmental process.

A detailed study (Lichtenberg & Knox, 1991) of four groups attempted to establish movement from random interaction patterns to a more structured process over the life of the group. The authors ". . . hypothesized that, to the extent that therapy group processes develop across the life of the group, group order and complexity would change to reduce chaos and to produce (and be reflected in) increasing structure" (p. 280). The analysis failed to support a structural developmental process, and found little change in the interaction patterns of the members and leaders from the beginning to the end of the group.

A related suggestion (Yalom, 1985) proposed that the developmental stages of groups are related to particular therapeutic factors. If there is a relationship between the group's maturation and particular curative elements, movement through these stages may be facilitated by emphasizing specific therapeutic factors at certain points in the group (Waldo, 1985).

Kivlighan and Hullison (1988) attempted to relate developmental processes to curative factors in the group. In general they found that the members perceived acceptance, learning from interpersonal actions, universality, and insight equally important in the first half (sessions 1–5) of the group. LIA became more important in the second half (sessions 6–11), while acceptance and insight continued to be seen at about the same level of prominence throughout. Guidance and altruism were viewed as being relatively insignificant influences across the life of the group, while the rest of the factors were of moderate importance for all sessions.

GROUP BEHAVIOR IN DIFFERENT STAGES

Some theorists, in particular Zimpfer (1986), suggested that it would be quite useful for group analysis and planning to be related to the developmental phase of the group. The developmental scheme would need to be related to the leader's own style and theoretical orientation, but once chosen it would guide the design process. The advantages of a developmental approach includes the ability to understand more easily the current forces and behavior in the group, and how an individual's actions relate to the group's evolution. Once the group's stage of development is identified, the leader can plan strategies that will assist the individual member's learning, as well as facilitate the maturation of the group as a whole.

Despite a lack of overwhelming research evidence to support the existence of developmental stages, a working understanding of group phases is helpful. Although leaders may use different terms to describe the phases, it seems probable that groups do go through periods when their interpersonal behavior reflects concern with distinctive issues, such as the need for acceptance at the beginning of a group or the reluctance of members to terminate a positive group experience at the end. There seems to be general agreement about how the members behave during each stage. The following descriptions represent a reasonable schema of developmental stages, and they are related to therapeutic factors whenever possible.

Beginning Stage

The early sessions of a group often reflect concern about acceptance and universality. Members are preoccupied with how the other participants view them, and how they fit in the group. A leader often witnesses individuals actively searching for commonalities, with a tendency to minimize differences. Self-disclosures mostly involve giving information about the self, as opposed to feelings about others or the group. Guidance activities may be frequent, and take the form of offering advice or suggestions, and trying to be helpful to each other. Advice or information is often offered primarily to gain the acceptance of the receiver, rather than as an act of altruism.

At times, the beginning may show a rather rapid superficial form of acceptance and universality. Members customarily seek to establish the most obvious similarities, or to admire the most obvious differences. Conflict is either avoided or quickly smoothed over if it should arise spontaneously. This early stage is notable for people trying to determine how (or if) they fit in, how the group will operate, and who has the influence other than the leader.

An essential conflict revolves around balancing needs for independence and dependence. Each person is examining (at some level) what will be the personal price for inclusion in the group, or "How much will I have to give, or give up, in order to get in?" This question, although inelegantly stated, asserts each person's primary struggle between dependence and autonomy. Most members want to use the group for positive benefit, but it will cost something, and will it be worth the cost?

Awareness Stage

Movement into the awareness stage is almost unavoidable. At some point each person will recognize that to make further gains means having to take risks of some type. If the decision to move forward is not made, the choice to remain at the beginning means there is little chance of much positive benefit from other members. People may become aware of the need to commit risk taking at different times. Even after there is awareness of the choice, people decide to move ahead at separate moments. The result of the uneven choices is to produce anxiety and conflict. Some participants want to move ahead, some do not, and others are ambivalent about the whole process.

The prime issues in this stage are still ones of acceptance and universality and they are being explored at a more realistic level as the group begins serious work. The superficial acceptance of the first phase has given way to behavior which will test how others "really feel about me." Self-disclosures move to more sensitive material and more honest and direct interpersonal feedback ensues.

Direct challenges to the leadership often happen during this period. There is often disappointment with the leader not having fulfilled the member's fantasy of magic change with almost no effort. Now the leader's warts are visible. There is the disappointment that comes with recognizing the humanness of the leader, coupled with the relief that the leader is just like everyone else.

This stage can be quite troubling for leaders. Overt and covert conflict are present. Often, members are ambivalent about moving the group forward, and they may express confusion about what they want and what the group is to do. It is not unusual to have the complete extremes—one member encouraging everyone to get involved and another declaring the whole process is a "complete waste of time!" What makes it even more difficult for leaders is that none of the positive, negative, or ambivalent feelings may be expressed very directly at times. Expressing exactly how one feels is still too risky for some. This period of uproar will probably require the most careful analysis and thought of any period in the group's development.

Working Stage

Although there may have been substantial gains during the Beginning and Awareness stages, this phase provides the most opportunity for using the inherent positive dynamics of the group. Once a reasonable level of cohesion has been developed, most members participate in more personal types of self-disclosure and feedback, and that increases opportunities for meaningful catharsis, LIA, insight, and vicarious learning. Once work commences, a lot of gains are possible within a relatively short period of time.

The working phase, once entered, seems to represent a developmental sequence which is irreversible. The group may face threats to its solidarity, or experience significant conflicts, yet there has been agreement to attempt to work through it all. Participants have made a commitment which will carry the group forward. Many leaders use the description of a "cohesive group" to describe this phase. Even so, there may be a recycling between Awareness and Working stages as new issues arise and the level of commitment changes. For example, more personal self-disclosures create new risks for interpersonal acceptance, which have to be handled in the group. This recycling of issues typifies all major relationships in life, so it is not surprising to find it as a major element in a committed group.

Ending Stage

Ending stages are characterized by behavior which is similar to some of the ambivalence demonstrated in the Awareness phase. At one level, individuals want to express their autonomy by giving up the group, and at another level are afraid to do so. Consequently, they may resist its termination. There is probably a correlation between the length and/or intensity of the group and the strength of this feeling. Ideally this is a time to consolidate gains and to plan realistically for the transition from the group. At the same time, all the variety of feelings associated with separation and leaving arise. Members may express anger, sadness, feelings of abandonment or excitement about the future. Separation anxiety often will create themes that can be effectively used in the group's process.

Some groups tend to resist termination by introducing the idea of extending the process, or by planning post group social gatherings. As is true in individual therapy, old, and supposedly resolved, issues may be reintroduced as evidence that the person is not ready to leave.

Overall Process of the Group

One problem with the model just described, or any other that might be suggested, is that groups rarely exhibit a smooth developmental sequence. In Tuckman's (1965) terms, the fact that the group went through an intense period of Norming, followed by some active Storming and Performing, does not mean the group cannot find itself suddenly demonstrating early Forming behavior. As new issues arise, the stages (or mini-stages) may recycle repeatedly. For example, a person might feel accepted early in the group, but following a sensitive self-disclosure, feel rejected and withdraw from the interaction. The group may then demonstrate some patterns of behavior more associated with the early stages of the group until the member has been re-included.

Therefore, the natural evolution of a group requires some issues to be handled repetitiously as part of the ongoing group agenda. Issues related to acceptance, universality, and influence, for example, repeat themselves continually. This cyclic type of activity is one of the hallmarks of groups, and also one of the major reasons that definitive statements about "how groups work" is so difficult. The nature of groups cannot be understood easily from a scientific perspective which has been developed primarily for linear models oriented toward simple cause–effect relationships. At times it seems that chaos theory may provide a more definitive and helpful formulation for group work.

Obviously, the type of group, its length, and many other factors will affect the group's development. Long-term therapy groups naturally will show different patterns from ten session common-theme groups. The way the stages are described would also be affected by the theoretical orientation of the leader and the planned objectives of the experience. More research will undoubtedly create new models. As Zimpfer (1986) suggested, leaders are advised to use the developmental model which best fits their particular group.

4

LEADERSHIP FACTORS
AND STRATEGIES

Although specific leadership strategies will vary depending on the type of group, number of participants, and many other variables, there are some general factors and tactics which apply to almost any kind of therapeutic group. The commonality of therapeutic factors across a variety of groups suggests that there are known ways that leaders can act that promote the development of the participants. There are also leader actions which are likely to increase the risk of negative outcomes for the group members. Leaders need to be particularly careful when handling the resistant, or ostensibly deviant member.

LEADERSHIP FACTORS

Effective Group Leaders

It is tempting to list all the hypothetical personality requirements that might be associated with a good group leader. However, developing such a list provides little useful information. All the characteristics associated with being a decent therapist apply and descriptions of desirable leaders are readily available from any recognized theoretical school of counseling or psychotherapy. From another perspective, at least one theorist has suggested that group leaders ". . . seem generally more comfortable with self-display than therapists who prefer to work one to one." (Weiner, 1983b; p. 54).

A group therapist is certainly much more "on stage" than in dyadic work. Whether that fact supports the idea that leaders are more exhibitionistic or not, is an interesting point for discussion. Most leaders would choose to think that the attraction to group work is causally related to the continuing stimulation offered by the dynamics of the members. On the other hand, some practitioners of psychodrama certainly seem to have a flair for the theatre.

An attempt to compare the characteristics associated with successful individual and group therapists produced a few findings of interest. Although the two types of therapists cannot be distinguished by many factors, some authors feel that the group therapist tends to ". . . create a more egalitarian influence . . . ," admit mistakes, extend trust, and use humor (Fuhriman & Burlingame, 1990, p. 21).

For whatever reason, group leadership requires some excellent listening skills along with a willingness to tackle difficult interactions rather than avoid them. In their survey, Dies and Teleska (1985, p. 134) found that many experienced group therapists felt that:

> . . . the courage to deal with difficult clients in the group, to face potentially harmful group process, and to stand up to powerful group forces were prerequisites for effective group therapy.

In addition, there are a few other conditions leaders face which may be more difficult in group than dyadic work. The opportunities for distorted relationships (transference and counter-transference) are much greater simply because the leader is involved with a lot more people at the same time. There are more opportunities to get involved in a relationship which is not helpful to the client or the therapist. Most people find it difficult to monitor multiple relationships at the same moment. It is particularly difficult if the leader is working alone and has no help in observing the nature of the relationships.

The multiple associations in a group also make it more likely that one problem relationship can eventually influence and contaminate others. As the problem relationship intensifies, and related alliances form, there is the risk of members becoming entangled in a symbolic representation of one's family. As Yalom (1970) suggested, groups are excellent places to recapitulate one's family group and learn from it. The converse is another possibility—a person may also replay family pathology. Group leaders often find themselves entangled in the same drama, often acting in the role of a good or bad parent. Without careful and thoughtful action by the leader, there is not only a possibility that old family dramas may be reenacted in the group, but that they will remain unresolved. Obviously, co-leadership will help prevent such occurrences.

In the event of a negative family recapitulation, the solo leader can only hope for an astute supervisor, or a very psychologically aware group. Common-theme groups which utilize a brief therapy format are less likely to develop negative family systems, but they are not immune from it. The longer-term general therapy groups are more likely to manifest family reenactments and have more opportunities to profit from them. In the latter group, the family system can become the focus of the group, and become a source of considerable learning.

Interpersonal Style

There is another important personal aspect of leadership which can affect interpersonal interactions. Some leaders may have primary interpersonal issues which affect how they behave in groups. One way of viewing this behavior was developed by Schutz (1978) and integrates factors which might constitute at least a partial interpersonal style, or way of approaching people. The general pattern will be the same in a dyad or in a group and is heightened in a group. Schutz has suggested that we have three fundamental ways of relating which involve Inclusion, Control, and Affection (the ICA Model). The definitions and leadership implications for each factor are as follows.

Inclusion: the need to establish and maintain a satisfactory relationship with people; the need to like and be liked.

Leaders high on inclusion needs will be oriented toward relationships in the group, particularly their relative affiliation with each other person. Such leaders will want to be accepted by others, and may have a tendency to avoid conflict because of the possibility of rejection. They may avoid directive interventions because of the need to be liked. On the other hand, high inclusion leaders are very sensitive to needs for interpersonal acceptance. They are likely to expend a lot of energy ensuring that participants reach a minimum level of inclusion in the group. Group leaders whose predominant interest is being liked tend to work toward developing cohesive groups.

Control: the need to establish and maintain a satisfactory relationship with people by exercising control and power; the need to influence.

At moderate levels such people with control needs can be excellent leaders. However, if there is a combination of low inclusion needs and moderate to high control needs, the person can sometimes sacrifice interpersonal acceptance at the expense of running the group in accordance with the design. They would rather "be in charge" than have the approval of others. A risk for a high control leader is that the group moves quickly toward a specified goal, but the positive interpersonal resources never develop.

Affection: the need to establish and maintain a satisfactory relationship with others based on love and affection; a need for intimacy.

A very useful trait for the longer-term group, yet in short-term groups the person with high affection needs runs the risk of being continually frustrated, or forming close relationships that may not be based on a solid foundation. The leader with high affection needs may spend group time trying to facilitate intimacy and will probably fail to meet the needs of group members who do not have similar needs. Another risk for a leader who needs high levels of intimacy is the possibility of prolonging the group beyond the point where it is useful for some members.

These three factors should be considered relative to how much they are both *wanted* and *expressed*. *Wanted* refers to how important it is that others fulfill a particular need, and *expressed* refers to how much the person actualizes the need at a behavioral level. For example, a person could have a very high need for being liked by others (wanted) but do little to meet that need (expressed). People with a combination of high wanted—needs—but low expressed, are very likely to be frustrated in a group setting. They do not *act* to get what they want. More importantly, they are difficult for the leader to understand because they give few clues as to what they want out of the group.

Similarly, a leader with a significant discrepancy between wanted and expressed on a factor is likely to send unclear (non-congruent) messages to the participants. There are many other combinations of patterns, and it is helpful for leaders to have some idea of their basic interpersonal style and how it is reflected in a group setting. Although some reflection and feedback from others can be used effectively to determine an ICA pattern, it is more helpful to actually take and score the questionnaire. The FIRO-B Fundamental Interpersonal Relationship Orientation-Form B (Schutz, 1978) produces a profile on wanted and expressed inclusion, control, and affection. The ICA tabulation can be useful for providing clues about leadership styles in groups and other interpersonal situations. Of course the FIRO-B is only a rough measure of group leadership style and should be supplemented with observations in a relevant setting.

Regardless of whether the ICA Model is used, it is beneficial for leaders to perform a self assessment on their general relationship orientation in a group. Some therapists who are demonstrably warm and empathic in a dyad seem to become remote and controlling in a group. Other leaders seem stimulated by the group and become more interactive and engaging than they normally are. A careful assessment of style helps pinpoint which personal strengths and weaknesses appear in a group situation, and feedback from a coleader and group participants is probably the most effective way to conduct the self-appraisal.

Coleadership

Although there are few studies which have compared sole and coleadership, there are some reasons to endorse coleadership as a preferred way of running groups. Dual leadership *may* require more time commitment, but the benefits are well worth the extra time. Advantages for coleadership include the following:

1. There is an additional perspective on both individual and group dynamics. Two leaders can offer more opportunities for learning for each person or for the group as a whole. For example, one leader can take primary responsibility for leadership while the other observes the interactions.

2. Interpersonal distortions, particularly strong reactions, can be clarified and addressed. Without a coleader to help, such a

situation can be risky for the participant. When a participant and a leader are in conflict, or are participating in unhelpful patterns of interaction, there is another trained person who can help to remediate the situation. Coleadership is a particularly good way of trying to prevent negative outcomes—or real casualties.

3.   Coleaders provide much better opportunities for therapeutic alliances. What happens, for example, if a single leader cannot form a good working relationship with a particular member? If another professional is present in the group there is another opportunity for the member to form a working alliance.

4.   There is insurance for the group in case one leader becomes ill, has a family emergency, or is late for a group. The group can continue to meet and function in such circumstances.

5.   There are some group situations in which coleadership is mandatory. At times coleaders of both genders are thought to be essential, such as when the group is composed of children of divorced parents (Lesowitz et al., 1987). Groups composed of men who have molested children seem to benefit by having male-female coleaders. A female coleader is essential for creating useful reactions, and the two leaders can model appropriate male-female interactions (Pietz & Mann, 1989). In other situations, such as in groups with heterosexual couples, abused children and parent groups, coleadership seems to be preferable.

6.   Another circumstance where coleaders are necessary is when a common-theme group is composed of people with a complex medical condition. Many illnesses require consistent work with psychosocial concerns *and* accurate input from physicians or other knowledgeable health professionals. Guidance activities are important for some conditions and many psychologists cannot respond accurately or ethically to some physical concerns that patients might have.

Additional benefits for using two leaders include the opportunity to model interpersonal interaction, compensate for the other therapist's shortcomings, and general enrichment of the group experience (Dies & Teleska, 1985). Sharing leadership is recommended as an excellent way of learning and having a ready support person available, which helps avoid burnout. The support function cannot be overemphasized, particularly when the group is going through difficult phases of development. Even though coleadership may seem to be less efficient, it is well worth the extra use of professional time.

One explicit assumption underlying the recommendation to colead is that the two leaders have compatible or complementary styles of interacting. As Dies (1983a) suggested, incompatible leadership methodology may actually create more problems than single leadership. A common sense approach is recommended. The two leaders should be able to communicate well and show that they like each other. If at times they disagree, they should have the capacity to work through the problem without creating excessive tension or conflict in the group.

If a coleadership condition is not possible, then it is strongly recommended that the leader arrange for supervision. As is true with any therapeutic endeavor, ongoing consultation almost always is helpful. Having someone to talk to after difficult sessions can assist the leader to maintain a useful perspective.

LEADERSHIP STRATEGIES

Another prerequisite for effective group leadership is some overall conceptional scheme about why and how groups work (Anderson & Robertson, 1985). Leaders need a model which guides how they think about group process and what types of interventions might be useful in a given situation. Without some clear theoretical system, the leader can model interventions which have no coherence, and could confuse the members. A number of leadership models have been used to describe helpful patterns of behavior.

In their study of encounter groups, Lieberman, Yalom, and Miles (1973) attempted to determine which types of leader activity were related to positive and negative outcomes by their participants. The research involved 17 leaders and about 200 participants. The leaders were highly trained, experienced, and represented a variety of theoretical orientations. The leader's behavior in the group was monitored by observers and assessed by questionnaires. The subjects were evaluated on pre- and post-measures, and completed a follow-up assessment after six months. Positive and negative outcomes for participants were correlated significantly with clearly identifiable leader behaviors irrespective of the theoretical emphasis of the leaders. The researchers were able to identify four major dimensions of leadership, which were (1) emotional stimulation, (2) caring, (3) meaning-attribution, and (4) executive function.

Emotional stimulation referred to a prominent emphasis on confrontation, expressing feelings, and risk taking. Leaders high on this factor modeled high levels of participation and expression of feelings. These leaders exhibited and promoted risk taking, self-disclosure and cathartic experiences were encouraged.

The second factor, *caring*, referred to leader actions which protected members, sought friendship and gave affection. The caring leader emphasized support, praise, and encouragement. This leader tried to create conditions where therapeutic factors such as acceptance and universality could develop.

Meaning-attribution refers to ". . . cognitizing behavior—providing concepts for how to understand, explaining, clarifying, interpreting, and providing frameworks for how to change (p.238)." These leaders often intervened with reflections or explanations which offered new insights to the individual or the group. They strived to create opportunities for learning from interpersonal actions. In other words, these leaders put behavior in a context so it could be generalized and extended to other circumstances.

The fourth factor, *executive function* described a management activity. The leader acted to set limits, suggest goals, or offer suggestions to a participant or the group as a whole. They are seen as directors, ". . . stopping the action and focusing on a particular behavior either of the group or an individual." (p.239). Executive functions provided the structure and direction for the group, an activity strongly endorsed by advocates of brief therapy (Burlingame & Fuhriman, 1990).

After extensive analysis, the four clusters of leader behavior were correlated with positive outcomes by participants. The following relationships were obtained:

Leadership Factor	*Correlation with Positive Change*
Emotional stimulation	.24
Caring	.60
Meaning-attribution	.70
Executive function	.20

In general, emotional stimulation and executive function were found to be curvilinear. Leaders who were very low or very high on the two dimensions were unsuccessful. Caring affected the group in a very predictable way; the more the leaders demonstrated caring, the better the outcome. High levels of meaning-attribution were correlated positively with desired change, and low levels were associated with a lack of success. Creating high levels of experiential encounters, as in catharsis, did not appear to precipitate much change. There was clearly a necessity that the leader connect events in the group with a conceptual framework.

Finally, the authors analyzed several patterns of the four dimensions and a topology of group leadership was developed. By far the most successful leaders were classified as *providers*. These leaders demonstrated high levels of caring and meaning-attribution and used moderate levels of emotional stimulation and executive function. Providers ". . . gave love, as well as information and ideas about how to change, and they exuded a quality of enlightened paternalism. They subscribed to a systematic theory about how individuals learn which they used in the group but did not press" (p.243).

Translating the provider pattern into therapeutic factors suggests:

1. An emphasis on acceptance, demonstrated by warmth, active support, and genuine concern by the leader. Universality and self-disclosure are important as a further way of bonding the leader with each member, thus increasing the level of acceptance. The self-disclosure is not a recitation of fact or history and primarily indicates feelings of liking and support toward the members.

2. In addition to ensuring high levels of acceptance, a major function of the leader is to offer a variety of ways to increase the levels of insight and LIA. Behavior in the group needs to be labeled and organized in a way which provides a conceptual format, or scheme, for the members to follow. The type of model does not appear to be important, as long as the participant understands and uses what is being offered. Whatever model the leader uses needs to be clear to all the participants, but should be *offered* only, not imposed.

3. It is also likely there is a clear correspondence between insight and LIA. The interactions in the group provide data for both insight and learning new ways of behaving. The leader's observations of individual and group behavior as it happens provide the basis for new learning.

Based on their conceptual model, effective leaders emphasize acceptance and offer an intelligible model for change. They offer useful observations about individual and interpersonal behavior which are clearly related to the leader's change model.

A slightly different yet overlapping model was provided by Anderson (1985). He felt there were four major styles of leader behaviors and defined the functions as: (1) providing—primarily a relationship variable where the leader sets a positive climate via support, concern and acceptance; (2) processing—this factor refers to supplying meaning and a conceptual framework for understanding and change; (3) catalyzing—promoting interaction in a variety of ways; and (4) directing—a group management function.

Another extensive study on leadership was conducted by Mackenzie et al. (1987) at one of the annual American Group Psychotherapy Association (AGPA) Institutes. The 1982 Institute consisted of 54 small groups, of which 28 represented specific interest groups and 26 general groups. The groups met for 14 hours over two days. A variety of measures were used to evaluate both the process and outcomes of the experience. The participants were asked to rate the leaders on a list of 40 adjectives and the results were factor-analyzed. The analysis produced five factors, of which three were positive and two negative. The factors and some representative adjectives are listed below:

Factor	*Descriptions*
Caring	Accepting, caring and empathic
Charismatic	Brilliant, inspiring and stimulating
Skillful	Knowledgeable, skillful and perceptive
Inhibiting	Defensive and negative
Controlling	Manipulative and controlling

The eight most highly rated groups were compared with an equal number of the least successful groups. The most effective groups had leaders who were rated significantly higher on the first three factors, that is, *caring, charismatic,* and *skillful.* The *caring* factor was by far the most important and was associated with groups that had relatively positive outcomes. As might have been expected, those groups rated as least successful had leaders described as significantly more *inhibiting,* and higher on the *controlling* factor.

One interesting finding was that 7% of the members of the most highly rated groups ranked their experience quite low on the scales. Similarly, 4% of the participants in relatively unsuccessful groups felt their experience was quite beneficial. Apparently, despite the leader's good or bad efforts, there were some members who perceived their group quite differently from the rest of the participants. The reasons for the discrepant ratings were unknown, although the authors speculated that transference issues may have been the cause.

A different perspective on leadership was offered by Yalom (1985). He described leadership in a sequential manner which was associated with three basic tasks for the leader.

1. There is the creation and maintenance of the group, which involves the selection and preparation of the members, setting time and place for the meeting, and essentially getting the process started. Once the group is underway, a major function for the leader is to attend to the integration of new members and the general cohesiveness of the process. Behavior which threatens the integrity of the group must be handled first, and at times, the needs of an individual member are secondary.

2. Therapists must create an environment where serious work can occur and this process is called "culture building" (p.115). A major part of culture building is the development of norms for the group. The group generates sets of operating rules which eventually govern the interaction. The development of a group culture is linked naturally to the development of therapeutic factors, particularly encouraging such factors as acceptance, universality, altruism, and self-disclosure. Yalom felt the leader should attempt to develop a group that may act to cause change in the participants, rather than depending on the therapist to be the primary initiator of transformation.

3. Leaders should use the here-and-now experiences of the participants in a way that promotes change. One of the major ways the group illuminates the present is through a processing of itself, that is ". . . the group lives in the here-and-now, and it also doubles back on itself; it performs a self-reflective loop and examines the here-and-now behavior that has just occurred." (Yalom, 1985; p. 136).

This collective self-reflection allows the members to separate the process from the content. The self-reflection becomes far more than a repeat of the verbal content and extends the group's awareness of interpersonal behavior and its consequences. The process analysis provides the participants with a more objective view of the interactions in the group, and provides opportunities for individuals to learn about themselves. The "doubling back" process produces opportunities for insight, LIA, and other curative factors to develop.

Drum (1990) described a leadership model which has some similarity to Yalom's, and is applicable to thematic groups. His design involved four elements: the creation of a therapeutic environment; interpersonal process management; examination of intrapersonal factors; and structuring procedures. Each major factor contains sub-elements and strategies that can be emphasized or minimized, consistent with the design and focus of the planned group.

In contrast to the longer-term outpatient general therapy group, time-limited approaches sometimes require changes in leadership style. Most common-theme groups require more focused approaches. Dies (1985, p. 436) recommended that short-term therapy groups should emphasize a "problem-focused, present-oriented, and positive approach to conflict resolution." The leader of brief groups is seen as a technical expert, who actively creates optimal learning environments for the participants. Leader activity involves such actions as structuring and facilitating a supportive and accepting environment. In addition, therapists need a conceptual model which supports the use of a particular process or intervention. In this model the group operations become a totally open process, and the participants are informed about the rationale for how the group is conducted.

Summary of Leadership Functions

- Strongly facilitate interpersonal acceptance.
- Provide high levels of caring and support whenever possible.
- Develop a clear model to promote insight and LIA.
- Offer a change model but do not impose it.
- Actively manage the process.

- Use the group process as a primary tool for learning.
- Relate the current process to overall goals.
- Take responsibility for creating a therapeutic environment.

HUMOR IN GROUPS

Humor in a therapeutic situation is rarely planned, except perhaps for Farrelly's work with provocative therapy (Farrelly & Brandsma, 1974). At his best, even Farrelly's work reflected a spontaneous natural flow rather than following a deliberate plan. Many therapists have begun to utilize natural forms of humor quite effectively (see for example, Fry & Salameh, 1987). Many people come to therapy because they take themselves too seriously. Sometimes there is the temptation to oblige them by agreeing that the problem *is serious* which often assists the entrenchment of the difficulty. Instead, using humor to defuse the "heaviness" of a problem can be quite effective (Bloch, 1987).

Group situations provide many opportunities for humor. Tuttman (1991) discussed the appropriate and inappropriate uses of humor in psychodynamic group work. He felt that humor can be used most effectively to assist with insight, in dealing with resistance, and facilitating individuals in working through problems. He did warn, however, of the destructive potential of humor. Due to the possibility of transference-countertransference reactions, the leader needs to monitor carefully when and how humor is employed.

Napier and Gershenfeld (1981) also have recommended several humorous strategies, including noting paradoxes within the group, overstating universal truths, and being aware when the miserable view is becoming the norm during the discussion. In the latter case, people who take a depressive view of most situations are often effectively handled by vigorously adopting their perspective. A healthy and humorous exaggeration of how awful their life is can help them consider a new position. Many leaders have found that agreement with a person's miserable perspective produces an argument. The client begins to assert that "Things aren't that bad!" which produces an effect recommended by Farrelly and Brandsma, (1974).

Leahey and Wallace (1988, p. 214) reported some interesting examples of the strategic use of humor in self-esteem groups.

Group members were sometimes asked to role-play such out-rageous events as a "pity party" or a "bitter party" and decide such issues as who to invite to the party, what type of food should be served, who should never be invited . . . , and what kind of conversation to have. Other examples included role-playing ten different ways to say "I'm sorry".

There are some valid concerns to be considered before the wholesale use of humor in groups is recommended. As is true of any significant incident in therapy, the use of humor needs some kind of post-hoc review. Using humor as a cover for other, more difficult messages is not an effective communication device. Sarcastic comments can get a laugh, yet often are indirect ways of expressing anger. When the leader uses humor as a covert way of expressing anger, seductiveness, or power, clients can be harmed.

Humor also can be used inappropriately to avoid uncomfortable issues, especially in groups. Awkward, uncomfortable situations can be defused by a quip, rather than encouraging the group to deal with the anxiety in the situation. It is common for group participants to use humor to avoid sensitive issues, gain attention, or to be covertly aggressive. Like any other human action, humor can be analyzed only by its appropriateness in the context in which it is used.

Although the most positive therapeutic results probably will result from humor which arises spontaneously, in some groups humorous exercises might be used profitably. In particular, designs which attempt to create humorous paradoxes seem to have good therapeutic potential.

PROBLEM SITUATIONS

Often, group leaders are faced with problem members or circumstances which require active intervention. Knowing when and how to intervene is difficult and the leaders need to be clear about their motivations *prior* to taking action. Kline (1990) recommended a specific process for interceding which largely avoids the risk of harm to the person. When considering an intervention, the leader should explore a series of questions.

1. What am I feeling, and how intense are the feelings? Intense feelings are often signals that the leader's own issues are involved, and consultation with a colleague probably is needed. Also, interventions are not likely to be very effective when they are associated with strong affect. The intensity of the feelings needs to be reduced prior to the actual intervention.

2. What evidence do I have that other members may have similar thoughts and feelings about the situation? Taking the time to observe, listen, and check perceptions helps clarify whether the dilemma is a problem for the leader or the whole group.

3. Which specific words or actions are related to my feelings, and what meanings do they have? Once the leader has some ideas about the specifics of his or her responses, the perception can be tested in the group. The person, or the group, can be given feedback and asked to comment on the accuracy of the observation. For example, if a person seemed to avoid intimacy, a comment such as "I noticed that several people in the group made some very positive overtures to you, and you responded with sarcasm each time. I wonder if you are uncomfortable when people reach out to you?"

If the leader can verify the reality of the problem and clear personal feelings, then more effective mediation of the problem is possible.

Situations Which Require Interventions

Some occurrences certainly require active interventions by the leader in order to keep the group process helpful, and to protect the integrity of the participants (Anderson & Robertson, 1985).

a. Domination occurs by individuals or cliques.

It is natural for some people to dominate discussions, or for members to form alliances with each other. In either case, the leader cannot allow the person or the alliance to stifle open discussion within the group. Less assertive members may be reluctant to confront the highly verbal member or the powerful subgroup without assistance from the leader. In some occasions, a member may see what is happening and bring the situation to the attention of the group. At other times the leader will have to initiate the confrontation. The form of the confrontation should be descriptive, and state observations about what is happening. The comments would not establish blame and simply point out patterns of interaction.

b. An opportunity arises for a relatively quiet member to participate.

The leader needs to carefully monitor the contributions to seek opportunities to include the shy or quiet person in the interaction. Nonverbal reactions can be noted, and the person encouraged to share reactions verbally. The leader may have to design exercises which allow the quiet member to speak in smaller groupings. If necessary, the leader can discuss the situation individually with the person and attempt to work out a contract which encourages more participation.

c. Group norms are changed without open discussion.

When the group has agreed upon operating rules, they may decide spontaneously to change the guidelines, particularly when a predicament arises which makes the old norms difficult to enforce. In such cases it is the leader's responsibility to ensure that the group is aware of what is happening, and to promote open discussion about the change. This problem represents another situation where the leader can be descriptive about what is happening without blaming individuals.

d. Members frequently focus on outside events.

One of the major advantages of working in a group setting is the availability of interpersonal interactions for learning. However, direct processing of current transactions can be uncomfortable for members. The leader needs to help the participant use the current interpersonal behavior of the group as much as possible for learning. Active leader observations can show members how to create opportunities for learning from interpersonal actions.

e. Participants do not use an effective feedback model.

In difficult situations group members may, for example, label others, make sweeping generalizations, or project their thoughts and feelings to someone else. Effective interpersonal communication models can be taught and reinforced so that learning from feedback can occur.

f. Events occur which may be detrimental to the individual or group.

Leaders cannot allow unpleasant situations to be ignored or avoided. Most people have experienced considerable social conditioning which allows them to ignore uncomfortable interactions, such as when people dislike each other. One of the major goals for many groups is to learn more constructive interpersonal behavior. The leader's support and direction may be needed to accomplish such an objective. Many negative interactions need to be processed clearly and effectively. Patterns of conflict can be replayed, analyzed, altered, and adapted, if necessary. How much a group chooses to focus on interpersonal differences is largely a function of the design; however, disruptive relationships need to be reconciled if at all possible.

Although effective interpersonal communication processes can do much to alleviate unproductive conflict, the participants may have to learn to live with some dissension. Reconciliation may be possible, but complete agreement cannot always be achieved. "Agreeing to disagree" and similar understandings can allow the group to continue its productive work. The idea of continual mutual harmony is as unrealistic in a group as it is in normal daily living.

Particularly in brief common-theme groups, the leader cannot intervene in all the issues that arise in the group. Some personal and interpersonal concerns have to be ignored because of the type of group, or the time available. If the conflict creates undue group tension, that is another matter. In many situations however, the recognition that two group members are not particularly fond of each other may not be addressed directly if each member has adequate support from the leader and other members. The art of leadership often involves compromise between individual and group needs. Learning which issues can be ignored, and which interactions have to be addressed is always requires clinical judgement. There are, however, some process issues so important they cannot be ignored. In particular, issues associated with basic interpersonal acceptance must be addressed.

Resistance and Conflict

Despite a careful intake process and a well-conceived design, there still will be situations where a group member will not easily adapt to the group. The apparent misfit then becomes a problem for the leader, and the rest of the group. Such people often are called by a variety of names, such as "monopolizer," "denier," "passive-aggressive," and other pejorative terms. These labels imply some form of resistance by the participant, meaning that the person is a group dissident. In some way the person refuses to conform to the norms the group has established. Most cases of resistance have little to do with any inherent need on the part of the member to disrupt the group and probably more to do with the natural conflict that arises between individual functioning and group norms. In fact, the use of the label "resistance" does much to exacerbate the problem, because it implies that the difficulty somehow resides with the person and not the group dynamics. The nature of groups inevitably produces conflicts and the natural style of many individuals can come into conflict with ordinary group norms.

> *Leaders need to accurately appraise whether the source of resistance is members' fears or ineffective leadership. Simply labeling a member "resistant" is to entrench this resistance even more deeply. A leader who shows willingness to explore and understand members' resistive behavior increases the likelihood of cooperation and risk taking (Corey & Corey, 1987, p. 142).*

Groups are inherently paradoxical; conflict between the individual and the group is inevitable. For example, leaders often implicitly or explicitly ask people to participate in meaningful self-disclosures in group. However, participants cannot determine what the group (or the leader) thinks a real self-disclosure is until after they have self-disclosed! Another example is the common belief that members need to learn to trust the group. In order to *demonstrate* trust, the member must attempt a revelation that is "sensitive" or difficult to talk about. For instance, the person may choose to reveal material that risks a negative response from the other members. If the self-disclosure is met with supportive comments, all may be well. If the disclosure produces negative feedback, the participant may feel rejected and decide other self-disclosures are too risky. An attempt to trust may lead eventually to increasing the feelings of mistrust. The inherent paradox associated with many desirable group behaviors means, for some individuals, intrapersonal conflict is not only inevitable, but ongoing.

Additionally, many wanted group behaviors come directly into conflict with normal individual needs. Consider the following excerpt from a group meeting.

"Humor is a defense mechanism, Hank," leader Marya said. "Why are you scared?" she asked, her blue eyes blazing sincerely.

"I guess I'm afraid the group won't like me as much if I tell them I think we're wasting our time."

"Right," said Marya, smiling with encouragement.

"You're not sharing with us, Hank," Marya said after a while. She smiled, "You don't trust us" (Rinehart, 1971, p. 398).

The dialogue is from a work of fiction which satirizes therapeutic endeavors of all kinds and the behavior of the leader is uncomfortably familiar. She has illustrated clearly the effect of wearing perceptual blinkers. By being so focused on a certain type of self-disclosure, she has missed the obvious one that did occur.

As the previous illustration shows, often it matters whether the new self-disclosure simply is providing new information about oneself or commenting on the group or process in general. Usually, groups are receptive to new personal information that a member self-discloses. Unfortunately a person who offers negative feedback about the group's avoidance or scapegoating (for example) is often not well received. The nature of the response may be outside the current norms of behavior in the group and the group or the leader may symbolically "kill the messenger." Many of the unwelcome communications arise from the conflict between individual and group needs, as the dialogue demonstrated.

When the two needs conflict, the leader can assist by pointing out the conflict and illuminating the group's response to it. If the group is allowed to repress or discount criticism then a dangerous norm has been generated. If such conflicts are viewed as an expression of the inherent paradox of groups, rather than as a threat, creative growth becomes much more likely. The resultant friction is viewed as constructive, rather than resistant (Smith & Berg, 1987).

At a practical level, most difficulties arise from leadership problems rather than a member's character deficit. The ICA Model (Inclusion, Control, and Affection) can be a helpful system for analyzing problems with members whose behavior appears to be inconsistent with the rest of the process. In general, a person who opposes a system *is not included in the system.* Such a person is simply operationalizing the paradox just discussed. Stated another way, if an individual does not feel accepted by a group the person will not give the group any control, and will not tend to go along with the group norms. The following case study illustrates a common form of what is often viewed as resistance.

Vincent

Vincent was a 45-year-old male who had appeared at an outpatient treatment center for alcoholics. During the intake process he denied a drinking problem and stated that he was here to "get his wife off his back." He did agree to participate in an education and group program composed of problem drinkers. Vincent sat rather silently through the first group meeting. Early in the second group he announced that based on what he had heard he "didn't really belong here." The group pressed him and he admitted serious marital conflict and two drunk-driving charges, yet insisted that such difficulties were common to a lot of people and didn't mean "I am an alcoholic." The group attacked his arguments even more strongly and Vincent became more angry and defensive. At this point the leader intervened and expressed support for Vincent's position. The leader stated that Vincent had the right to decide whether or not he was an alcoholic, or whether he had any problems with drinking at all. Furthermore, the leader agreed that maybe Vincent should not be in the group. He suggested that Vincent just continue to "Sit back, listen, and evaluate his own situation." The leader then noted that the group really had tried to be helpful from their own perspective, but that some of their experiences and observations might not fit Vincent at all.

Vincent's situation represents a common dilemma for leaders. Vincent denied commonality with the other participants who had established previously a norm. ("We're all alcoholics.") Therefore the group is threatened or angry about a denial that contradicts their norm. They attempt to bring Vincent back into line with the norm. Vincent's history of marital conflict and multiple drunk-driving offenses provided an invitation for the leader to agree with the group and label him a "denier." However, attacking the client's refusal to accept the implicit norm of the group usually leads to more defensiveness and risks a negative outcome. The client is not willing to adopt the norm of "We are all alcoholics," to be included in the group. Vincent may feel threatened by the group norm because he is not ready to reach such a conclusion about himself (assuming it is a valid deduction in the first place). So he expresses his lack of inclusion with increased control, as in "I'm not an alcoholic," meaning "You are not going to have any influence over me." In fact, it does not matter whether Vincent has a problem or not. He is clearly saying that now, in this group, he will not go along with the program. If the leader responds to Vincent's actions as a threat to his or her control, little gain for anyone is likely.

In this case the leader took a much wiser and safer course. Whether or not Vincent declares himself an alcoholic or not is Vincent's issue, not the leader's problem. Vincent's denial (if it is) is a problem of interpersonal behavior, not a challenge to be overcome. The leader has several potential traps. If a leader feels threatened by Vincent's behavior, he or she may try to convert him, side with the group against him, or simply attach a negative label to him. ("You're in denial!") Any of these strategies would have a high probability of failure for Vincent and the group. In this example, the leader was not threatened by Vincent, so it was possible to support him, and relieve the group pressure for him to conform.

The leader's support also makes it almost impossible for Vincent to fight about the issue. The suggestion that he sit and listen, and make his own decision, invites Vincent to move out of the interaction and gives him control of the situation. The obvious paradoxical components of the intervention placed the leader in a "no lose" interaction. Vincent can now sit and feel alright about himself, or not return for the next meeting if he chooses. There is no loss of face; he has been supported in his view by the expert. On the other hand, the leader's support also allows Vincent to move toward a more careful examination of his behavior because none of his energy needs to be employed in defense. So if Vincent sits and thinks, the leader wins, or if he moderates his position, the leader also wins. Most importantly, Vincent cannot lose either.

Finally, the leader ends the conflict by supporting the group's attempt to be helpful. He also makes a clear statement about the inappropriateness of their assumption that everybody in the group is alike. Although the majority might not like it at the time, the leader has sent a clear message that unpopular stands *will* be supported, which is crucial for feelings of safety and promoting risk-taking. Depending on the type of group, there also could be some real opportunities for learning via insight or LIA for the participants about their reactivity to Vincent.

In any case, the strategy for working with individuals like Vincent is similar and consistent with what attention to therapeutic factors might suggest. *Affirm the resistance.* In many cases supporting the resistance causes it to disappear. Assuming good selection procedures, most obstinacy in groups is a product of the participants not feeling accepted. The basic strategy of affirming the resistance can be applied to almost any problem. Silent members are told it is permissible not to talk until they are ready; verbose members are supported and taught more appropriate ways to assist the group, not subtly told to shut up; and angry members gain support for their grievances.

Referring to the previous discussion of paradox in groups, one way of approaching the process is to live with the tension rather than resolving it. As the case of Vincent demonstrated, there is no complete resolution, only differing needs. Vincent needs to be in control and retain his individuality, and the group needs cohesion and maintenance of its norms. Both needs can be respected, but a resolution at the time of the conflict may not be possible without creating a win-lose situation. If Vincent remains in the group, the tension will remain.

> If the group is unable to treat that conflict as a central and desirable part of its experience and instead relegates it to the "intolerable" or "to be obliterated" domains of the group, then the preconditions for development and growth are being eliminated (Smith & Berg, 1987, p. 654).

An Interactional Perspective on Resistance

Another way of handling difficult problems, as well as promoting interpersonal learning, involves looking at the behavior from an interactional perspective. Frequently, repetitious patterns of behavior are designed to produce specific types of consequences. A way of behaving often invites a predictable response. Anger begets anger or defensiveness, sadness solicits sympathy, denial invites attack, and so forth (Lewis, 1987).

The leader can be alert to situations where members are setting up negative interactional patterns, and the first clue is how the leader responds to the person's behavior. Leaders can "feel" invitations to fight, feel sorry for someone, or to perform a rescue.

Once the individual response is identified, the next step is to understand what kind of reaction is invited by the participant. This query may be answered by observing how others in the group are actually reacting. When the pattern of interaction is clear, the leader can construct a response which interrupts the flow of prescribed action–reaction. In Vincent's case, the leader's affirmation, rather than criticism (which was the expected response) was an unexpected way of reacting. The unusual reaction offered the opportunity for Vincent to consider a new way of behaving.

Another alternative is to use process observations to handle the situation. The leader may stop the group process and point out to the rest of the group how much energy they were spending trying to convince Vincent he had a problem. The group can then be asked to reflect on why it was so important to them to change him. Besides giving Vincent some breathing space, such an approach allows other members to get much more in touch with Vincent's feelings, and possibly be more supportive and less attacking. Furthermore, if the group actually began to reflect on their own difficulty with admitting problems and how they behave when they are feeling scared, there is the opportunity for Vincent to relate to the discussion and consider his own actions nondefensively. A key to the whole process is the leader's ability to recognize his or her reactions and work through them sufficiently to make a helpful intervention.

Another concern is that in interchanges with people labelled in some form as "resistant," the leader may collude with other members in creating a scapegoat. Negative collusion is much more likely to occur in situations where the therapist's own countertransference is part of the dynamics. Perhaps more regrettably, the patient's vulnerability may be not perceived at all by the leader.

Summary of Strategies for Handling "Resistance"

- Clarify your own thoughts and feelings about the person.
- Verify your perceptions.
- Keep the problem with you.
- Stay aware of the inherent individual versus group conflict.
- Try to understand what is really motivating the person.
- Sense the feeling which usually underlies the resistance.
- Support the person whenever possible.
- Clarify the interaction pattern that has developed.
- Consider refusing to respond in the expected way.

5

LEADERSHIP AND THE
THERAPEUTIC FACTORS

In addition to general leadership strategies, knowledge of the therapeutic factors enables the leader to increase the possibilities of positive change in the participants. If the ten curative elements are primarily responsible for change, then emphasizing their development is a sensible strategy.

The relationship between therapeutic factors and helpful group experiences is apparent. Group participants consistently report that specific curative elements are related to their positive changes (see Chapter 3). Acceptance, universality, insight, catharsis, and learning from interpersonal actions (LIA) have extensive support for their importance in a variety of group settings. Altruistic behavior and increased feelings of hope also positively influence people. Self-disclosure is probably a major part of any successful group; how it interacts with other factors is unknown. Offering accurate information or advice (guidance) is also very useful, particularly when the participants have physical problems and psychosocial concerns. Vicarious learning is not reported as an important factor and there is no evident reason for a leader to try to create such experiences. Spectator learning may occur at times, but planning for it is not an efficient use of time or effort.

Since therapeutic factors are associated with positive change, it makes sense for leaders to augment their development when at all possible. Focusing on particular factors at appropriate times in

stent with the model of brief group therapy. That
~ve and goal-directed in trying to use the group
~~ively. There are a variety of leader behaviors compat-
with a therapeutic factor as well as functional combinations
of factors. Translating the curative elements into both general and
specific leader strategies makes it more possible for the group
process to be effectively directed. This approach is compatible with
the suggestion that the leader use ". . . direct instruction, rein-
forcement, and modeling to build individual expectations and
group norms to support the therapeutic factors" (MacDevitt &
Sanislow, 1987, p. 77).

This suggested model of leadership is consistent with the general leadership strategies proposed by many researchers and clinicians. For instance, promoting the group's sense of cohesion means
facilitating the levels of interpersonal acceptance and universality.
Leaders who demonstrate high levels of "caring" behavior are perceived as more effective (for example, MacKenzie et al., 1987; Lieberman et al., 1973). Caring translates well into the therapeutic factor
of (leader) acceptance, meaning support *and* encouragement. Similarly, when leaders assist with meaning attribution ("cognitizing
behavior," Corey & Corey, 1987), they are primarily promoting LIA
and experiences of insight. In summary, the leader's attention to the
therapeutic factors offers opportunities for directly influencing constructive change in the participants. A leader may choose to emphasize certain curative factors at particular points in the life of the
group. An ongoing analysis of the group is essential to determine
when to emphasize which factors.

Each curative factor will be considered from the viewpoint of
which leader tactics might optimize its development. When appropriate, some factors will be illustrated with a case study.

ACCEPTANCE (COHESION)

*Acceptance relates to the individual's feeling of belonging,
interpersonal friendliness and valuing. Feeling understood
and supported usually is very important to each group member, and probably crucial for clients when they have revealed
sensitive material.*

The literature has suggested that a member's acceptance by
the leader and other members is important. This is particularly

true as a way of avoiding negative outcomes (Dies & Teleska, 1985). In general, as interpersonal acceptance increases it is likely that the frequency of learning opportunities increases also.

It is probable that the level of mutual acceptance is positively and consistently associated with other curative factors. The synergistic interaction involved with acceptance, universality, and self-disclosure probably produces the effects associated with increased cohesiveness. As intergroup acceptance and feelings of similarity increase, the level of self-disclosure will probably increase. Consequently, the group is seen as more "cohesive." A major difficulty is trying to determine a clear cause–effect relationship. Each variable reciprocally influences each other factor. "Cohesion" refers to multidimensional factors encompassing a variety of behaviors by all members of the group. Moreover, cohesion is perceived as an "atmosphere" or "mood" in a group, rather than something an observer can readily see, or quantify.

There may be some examples of group situations where it is not appropriate to foster interpersonal acceptance. Perhaps one exception is where the group members are in collusion with each other to avoid some threatening issue. Another form of inappropriate intermember acceptance involved Vietnam veterans who formed a premature cohesiveness that prevented the proper development of the group. Apparently a combination of factors, including the severity of combat stressors and the homogeneity of the group contributed to the effect (Parson, 1985).

Except in very unusual conditions, fostering acceptance is desirable. Acceptance needs to be considered from two viewpoints—acceptance by the leader and inclusion by each other member in the group. Due to the leader's stature in the group, feeling accepted probably is crucial for each member. At the same time, the leader needs to expend effort to ensure that intergroup acceptance is as high as possible. Most people begin the group with concerns about acceptance and are sensitive to how others see them. It is difficult for other factors to develop until the members feel some resolution of the inclusion issue.

Promoting Acceptance

The following examples of leader actions are suggestive and not exhaustive. Obviously, there is almost no limit to the creativity the leader can use to promote intermember acceptance. To increase the level of acceptance in the group, the leader can develop several tactics.

1. There is no better or easier way to facilitate acceptance than to demonstrate good listening techniques and note empathy in others.

Careful listening is an obvious task for a leader and its impact can never be underestimated. Active listening techniques provide evidence that the speaker is understood by the leader, or other members and is an excellent strategy. The leaders can show active support and note when other members have been verbally or nonverbally responding to the speaker.

2. Indicating how the person is unique provides evidence of acceptance.

Although people recognize and value commonalities with others, they want also to feel they are different. In fact, it is difficult to find two life situations which are identical, so the leader will have ample material to support a person's distinctiveness.

3. Provide support after a member has shared sensitive material which is important, as a demonstration of continuing affirmation of the person.

It is very important that the leaders be sensitive to their own reactions, and those of other members when a person has shared something she or he consider shameful. When a participant has talked about something for which they are blameless (for example, being abused as a child), it is usually not too difficult to offer support and acceptance. If the disclosure involves something which people normally condemn, such as criminal activity, affairs outside of marriage, or child abuse, the acceptance is more difficult to accomplish.

Clarifying personal reactions is important. If a person reported stealing from a charity, and the group expressed shock, the reactions cannot be avoided. The leaders will have to process their own reactions and assist the members to handle what they felt. Although such a situation is difficult, it provides the leader with a good opportunity to model effective and honest communication patterns.

A related problem arises when one person in the group is disclosing or behaving in a manner quite discrepant from everyone else. Without careful handling, atypical members can feel rejected by the group. Even worse, the rejection can eventually lead to a group "casualty." If the predicament is addressed early in the process, a leader often can modify the member's behavior, or provide enough personal support to prevent damage to the individual. If necessary the leader can work with the person outside the group. Some leaders are uncomfortable with individual meetings outside the group, yet it is preferable to a casualty inside the group. In longer term therapy groups, the group often develops the personal resources to manage a discrepant member without undue harm.

4. Reframing, or changing an attribution, is a very helpful strategy for encouraging acceptance.

Relabelling what the person is experiencing can be an effective strategy to promote acceptance. What one person might view as a failure to stay on a diet may be seen as "periodic opportunities to decide whether or not the diet is really that important." Another leader might reframe a dietary failure as "taking a break from the diet." Also, a leader can point out legitimately that many people would have given up after one failure, yet "You keep struggling and trying again." Obviously, the line between a reattribution and a rationalization is very thin. Nonetheless, almost any problem has at least one alternative perspective. Humor is effective with reframing, and adds to the potency of an intervention. A leader referred to a client's marital failure as providing a "good chance to re-evaluate your materialistic nature." Effective listening regularly provides information about how the problem or symptom "works positively" for the person.

5. Exercises to promote member acceptance are effective ways to build interpersonal acceptance.

Many members are reluctant initially to speak out in a group. The leader can design exercises which will create chances for members to talk in dyads or triads. The smaller group exercises allow shy individuals to develop relationships and feel supported in a less threatening way.

Despite the leader's best efforts, difficult problems of acceptance do eventuate. Handling such a problem can be particularly

troublesome when the group has allowed chronic patterns to develop, as illustrated in the following case study.

Case Study: Carl

Carl was a member of a group formed to work on mens'
issues, and to develop support networks. It was clear that
most of the members were unused to interacting with men
except through sports and business discussions. Almost everyone in the group reported receiving complaints from others
about poor communication.

From the very beginning Carl took the role of the group
clown. His largely sexist wisecracks were well received because the comments diffused anxiety. As the meetings progressed, Carl's behavior was increasingly seen as deviant
from the rest of the group, and the men became annoyed
with him. The leader's initial attempts to include Carl by
supporting his need to use humor to deal with tough issues
were unsuccessful. Carl avoided attempts to engage him in
any real work; he continued his refusal to deal seriously with
the concerns of the other men. Eventually, one of the dominant members confronted Carl. He told him that he ". . . was
acting like a clown, and to stop being an idiot." Most of the
group actively supported the confrontation and the others
passively acquiesced to it.

The leader quickly intervened and supported Carl's rights
and behavior. The intervention involved pointing out one of
the current (implicit) group norms, that is, joking about serious issues was not allowed. The leader contrasted the new
norm with the old one, when Carl was supported for using
humor to avoid difficult issues. Therefore, the group must
share some responsibility for his present behavior. Further, he
noted the group had asked Carl not to be a clown, instead of
telling him what they wanted him to be.

The leader went on to say that he had difficulty with
Carl's jokes at times, but liked his sense of humor. Other
members were able to eventually echo the leader's feedback.
The group later concentrated on talking about what behavior
they *did* want. Carl admitted that being a clown all the time
was not getting him what he wanted from the other mem-

bers. The leader effectively negotiated a contract for Carl to try some different ways of relating. When appropriate, the member who started the confrontation was also supported for risking his feedback to Carl.

Carl is an illustration of someone with problems of inclusion, who had not developed any techniques for getting past a joking level of intimacy. The group norms that initially supported Carl changed, putting him in an atypical position. In similar situations it is tempting for the leader to allow the confrontation and let the group "straighten Carl out."

Fortunately the leader could see the primary issue for what it was, one of control. Carl threatened the need of the other members to control the direction of the group. Once group norms are established, members will act to keep conduct within limits, even though the informal rules are not verbalized.

Carl's problem illustrates several principles related to inclusion issues and process. If a member does not feel accepted or does not know how to meet the new norms, they will persist in familiar patterns of behavior. Such behavior is a way of saying "If you don't like me, then I won't play your game." Then what may happen is the group expends more and more energy trying to bring the person into line and the person responds with increasing resistance. Without an effective intervention, the group either will actively reject or begin to ignore the person, an equally devastating form of rejection.

Another principle of importance is that the group needs to be directed at times to focus on what the members want, not what they *do not* want. The change in emphasis increases the opportunities for constructive feedback and contracting for change.

At no point in the process did the leader support dishonesty. The leader admitted his problems with Carl and could also honestly say that at times he did like his sense of humor. Anyone who was feeling as excluded as Carl probably was, would be very sensitive to attempts to manipulate him by false positive feedback. Honesty is no excuse for brutality. There is simply no real gain from avoiding personal reactions in the group because they are difficult to handle. If the interpersonal issues are not processed, then people are left to form their own conclusions about what is happening in the group.

For some types of common-theme groups, there may not be a lot of emphasis on interpersonal confrontation. The minor interpersonal controversy or disagreement can be left alone; however, where a member's basic acceptance by the group is in danger that is not the case. As Dies and Teleska (1985, p. 139) stated, "A sense of group cohesiveness and the experience of acceptance by co-members may protect most clients from experiencing harmful group effects."

Summary of Strategies for Increasing Acceptance

- Demonstrate accurate empathy.
- Note unique characteristics of members.
- Ensure support after a sensitive disclosure.
- Consider reframing problems in a more positive way.
- Design exercises that promote interaction.
- Keep the interaction as honest as possible.
- Retain the focus on what people want from others.
- Look for ways to affirm members who are not being accepted.

UNIVERSALITY

Universality arises when the group participant realizes that other members have comparable thoughts, feelings, or experiences. At a basic level, the feeling of "we are all in the same boat" is a description of universality.

An appropriate selection process helps begin work on universality. The members were selected because of their need to work on some common problem, and in some groups may be exclusively of one gender. Both factors would help the development of universality, but there is still work to be done. One of the objectives for any group is to decrease the members' feelings of isolation, and to realize other people have comparable thoughts and feelings. The development of universality is related closely to the preceding therapeutic factor—acceptance. The leader can promote universality by a number of methods.

1. Linking similarities between members as the group progresses is a useful strategy.

One effective opening is to state, for example, "You are here because you want to learn to manage your diabetes better. So you all have agreed that better management of the condition is one goal for the group." This opening statement addresses similar conditions and mutual goals. The leader then can ask each member to talk briefly about their diagnosis and aims for management. As each person contributes, the similarities are noted. As the sessions continue, there will be many opportunities to notice how the members are similar. Occasionally noting the linkages helps the members be more aware of their mutual situation.

Along with the verbal linking of common experiences, emphasizing the qualitative aspects of the common information or behavior assists in the change of attitudes (Latta, 1986). This strategy involves the leader encouraging people to talk about what they have experienced at more than the factual level. Participants relate more of the *quality* of what has happened to them, which has more of an impact on the listeners and allows for stronger identification.

2. Normalize thoughts, feelings, and behavior to foster universality.

A common report from many group members is they feel some experiences are unique and sometimes, shameful. Following a self-disclosure, people will volunteer similar feelings without prompting. If not, the leader can also invite comments with statements such as, "My hunch is that a lot of other people in the group get depressed about . . ." The leader can be alert for expressed similarities and offer them as themes for the group to consider. Feelings of universality increase when members see that their feelings of uniqueness or shame are familiar to others. The specific experiences people have undergone may differ, yet their responses to the events are often comparable. Knowledge of shared thoughts and feelings helps reduce the sense of isolation.

3. Groups often look for and express similarities by discussing common themes.

The most obvious way of creating themes is to state one that members share. For example, in the diabetics' group, the assertion that many people report that failing to stick to a diet produces anger toward themselves can be endorsed by other participants. This theme is used to initiate a discussion on how to manage self-blame. In fact, a significant part of the design process for common-theme groups is the identification of important topics germane to the group.

Universality is planned and promoted by creating themes for discussion. Predictable reactions to the identified problem are suggested and explored. For example, many treatment programs that follow the principles of Alcoholics Anonymous are organized on the "12 steps" utilized by people in recovery which is an example of creating universality by following common themes.

There are occurrences in a group when the leader notices that the discussion has focused on a topic. It is helpful to state the leader's perception of the theme and the participants' reactions. Common topics represent active examples of the participants' attempts to find or confirm a consensus. On these occasions the leader's observation can assist the development of the theme. The leader affirms the relevance of the theme and highlights it for discussion. At other times, noting that the group mood is angry, sad, or confused can move the members toward resolution as well as demonstrating they are "all in the same boat."

Of course, universally expressed feelings may not always be positive and in those cases the challenging of a theme may be desirable. When the group becomes stuck in helplessness or negativity, the leader may remind them of the position they have adopted. They are encouraged to reframe in a more positive light.

For example, in a group of people with diabetes there was considerable complaining about the perceived lack of control over their medication. Finally the leader said, "Everyone is saying that you can't have any control of your medication and there is *nothing* you can do about it." The leader's statement was both empathic and by emphasizing "nothing," provocative. The confrontation reminded the group in a helpful way that they were not taking responsibility for doing anything except complaining.

Sometimes, the efforts of a leader to promote universality produce unwanted effects, as the following case illustrates.

Case Study: Acting Out

A male school psychologist (perhaps unwisely) decided to form a group for adolescent males who had problems such as poor grades, disruptions in class, and a general lack of motivation. A group of six boys, aged 15–16, was obtained by referrals from teachers and after a brief meeting with each boy, all agreed to participate. There was some suspicion by the potential leader that the agreement to participate may have been because the boys could leave their classes to attend the sessions. However, since their absences would not seriously damage their academic standing, and would also give some relief to the teacher, he went ahead.

The first meeting began with each boy introducing himself and indicating why he was there and what he hoped to get out of the group. All the boys indicated some problems and hoped to "do better." The leader followed their comments with a statement about "hoping he could be helpful" and the usual admonitions about ground rules and verbal or physical abuse, and ended with a strong statement about confidentiality. In an attempt to get underway and promote universality, he then stated that it seemed that all of them shared a common problem of difficulty with teachers. The rest of the session evidenced general clowning around, discussion of the failings of their teachers and occasional references, with smirks, to the quantitative and qualitative value of various illegal substances. The leader faced a dilemma. Universality and acceptance were strongly evident in the group, unfortunately he was not part of either. When he tried to monitor the discussion, and create any order out of the chaos, the boys saw him as another controlling teacher and the whole process degenerated into a power struggle.

In subsequent sessions the leader did manage to salvage the group by resorting to a structure which still allowed the members freedom. The boys participated in "mock trials" weekly, where they could act as a jurors, defense or prosecuting attorneys, judges, and defendants. The defendant roles were structured so they represented issues. For example, one boy was charged with illegally quitting school, which led to a structured debate about the positives and negatives about continuing school. Other discussions focused on specific type of disruptive behavior, such as baiting teachers, joking in class, and fighting.

This approach allowed the boys to examine their implicit "consensus" on several issues without a lot of threat to an individual. By depersonalizing the roles, each boy was able to review some of his assumptions without openly risking a break with his peer group. Universality still existed at the overt level, yet change was made possible by removing the personal threat.

A more rigorous intake procedure probably would have prevented the initial problems with the group. There are also some leaders, given sufficient time, who could have moved the group ahead by process interventions only but this school psychologist did not feel confident about the possibility of doing so. This is an example of universality in the negative. Of course, it could be argued that the boys weren't really demonstrating universality at a "real" level but they were "in the same boat" operationally, as the leader discovered.

Summary of Suggested Strategies for Universality

- Plan for discussion of common themes.
- Use process observations to note the discussion of themes.
- Verbally link similarities between members.
- Normalize a participant's disclosure and invite comments.
- Note and challenge negative themes.
- Reduce the threat level in negatively homogeneous groups.

LEARNING FROM INTERPERSONAL ACTION (LIA)

LIA occurs when a person either initiates a new behavior or responds in a new way in the group.

The desired outcome of most therapeutic endeavors is evidence the person can do something that they could not do before, or desired action more frequently. One of the major advantages of a group is that it provides opportunities for new behavioral trials. New actions can be refined, and tried again. The new efforts provide a vehicle for shaping actions by the use of feedback. Using real interactions to learn is one of the most powerful learning resources available, and one of the major advantages of group work. There are several strategies which might provide opportunities for LIA.

1. Be aware of patterns of client behavior which evoke characteristic types of responses. Consider responding in a nontypical way.

As mentioned earlier in the discussion on resistance, many problem behaviors continue because the group and the leader continue to respond in the "expected" way. When members tend to repeatedly evoke boredom, confusion, anger, or pity, from others it demonstrates the presence of fixed patterns of interactions. In such circumstances there is a complementary nature to the transactions which helps maintain the maladaptive system. An effective technique is for the leader to model behaviors substantially different by reframing, or using paradoxical responses (Lewis, 1987). If, for example through the use of a reframing response, an individual's chronic anger or joking is seen as a cover for fear, the other members may respond differently and change the interaction pattern. If the leader can support a problem behavior rather than oppose it, the paradoxical response can alter the member's behavior.

2. Encourage and structure opportunities for trials of new thought patterns, behavior, and feelings.

There are many possibilities to begin and reinforce LIA, and the linking of thoughts, feelings, and behavior is a good beginning. For instance, a person may become aware that they make a lot of negative self-statements in response to a compliment. This awareness alone has little impact without the opportunity to practice making more positive self-statements in response to praise *and* behaving in a way congruent with the new thoughts. Normal group interactions provide many occasions for members to attempt different ways of thinking, feeling, and behaving if the three modalities are clearly linked.

3. Train people how to give feedback appropriately when interpersonal reactions are important for the design of the group.

When giving and receiving feedback is to be part of the process of a group, members need training in how to relate their reactions to others in a constructive manner. Many people do not know how to give useful feedback and use vague, evaluative, reactions instead. Effective feedback makes learning from interpersonal actions much easier.

Highly negative feedback understandably can create a potentially harmful experience, and should be discouraged. The leader should, at all costs, avoid any situation resembling "ratpacking" where several participants give negative feedback to another person in the group without corresponding support. Even mildly negative feedback is more effective if there is a level of positive trust or cohesion in the group first (Jacobs, Jacobs & Carior, 1973).

Ohlsen (1977) suggested some additional research-based guidelines for feedback including the ideas that (a) feedback which focuses on feelings rather than tasks is more effective; (b) feedback which addresses individuals rather than the group is preferred; and (c) positive feedback is more credible if the receiver knows the sender well. In other words, positive feedback early in a group frequently is viewed with suspicion. People, perhaps rightly, feel that if others do not know them well, how can others think they are so wonderful?

4. In groups where skills are taught, be sensitive to the person who might be significantly deficient in behaviors compared with the rest of the members.

Dies and Teleska (1985) raised concerns about the participant who has the group confirm their perceived inadequacies. Unfortunately, some of the same reasons that would make a person want to enter the group can increase the chances of a bad experience. A person with poor social skills who enters a group to learn how to make friends can be met with more rejections. In such cases, the leader may have to adjust the process of the sessions to provide necessary support and accommodate the deficient member.

5. Whenever possible, relate the person's actions in the group to similar external situations.

Although the group is not the real world in some ways, still it provides opportunities for situations which duplicate the normal environment. For example, if a person has difficulty speaking in the group, it is likely that the person has difficulty talking in analogous social situations. Characteristic ways of interacting tend to transcend environments. Longer-term therapy groups provide abundant opportunities for people to demonstrate their normal interaction style. As Yalom (1985, p.40) suggested:

Not only does the small group provide a social microcosm in which the maladaptive behavior of members is clearly displayed but also it becomes a laboratory in which they are demonstrated, often with great clarity, the dynamics of the behavior.

In some common-theme groups there are reduced chances for free interaction over long periods. The leader still can be alert for chances for generalization. The more a person's characteristic style of relating in the group is linked to situations outside, the better the chances for generalization. Any member can be asked to reflect on how current behavior is reflected outside the group environment.

Case Study: Patricia

A weight control group was advertised which would run for eight weeks, two hours per week. After intake interviews, six women and two men joined the group led by Bob and Carole. The primary objectives of the group were to provide weight control information, teach new self-control techniques and create readily available support systems for the participants.

Patricia was one of the more popular group members. She was enthusiastic about trying new methods and provided a lot of support for other members. Despite being a very busy homemaker with three young children, she was willing to listen to a member who wanted to call for support, or who needed transportation to an exercise class. It became obvious to the leaders that Patricia was putting considerable energy into the group, but she was not making any headway in her own self-management. They felt that one of the major reasons Patricia was not doing well was that she was "too available" to her family, the group members or whoever needed her. She did not make the time to follow her exercise program, practice relaxation, or to prepare foods that would help her stay on her diet.

The leaders decided to be alert for an opportunity to help Patricia look at her inability to "put herself first." An opportunity arose in the sixth session. The group was in the process of planning a social gathering over the following weekend where everyone would bring food, and there would be some sports activities. Such outings were encouraged as part of the design of the group. During the planning for the activity it became obvious that a place with a large yard would be necessary and someone remarked that Patricia's property was quite large. Patricia replied that her property was large enough, but the leaders noted that she did not really volunteer her place. However, the group continued the discussion and eventually someone stated that it looked like Patricia's place was best suited if that was alright with her. She answered in the affirmative, but not with much enthusiasm.

The group started to plan the specifics when Carole stopped the discussion and noted her observation that although Patricia had said "Yes," she seemed less than enthusiastic. Patricia looked a bit embarrassed, and said: "No, it would be alright to have it at her place." Carole again mentioned her lack of enthusiasm which was unusual for Patricia. After a bit of thought, Patricia admitted that her husband's parents were coming for a visit the day after the planned activity, and that she "was a nervous wreck when they came." Carole then stated, "It seems that Patricia feels that it would be very difficult for her to be a hostess for the social and then prepare for her husband's family the next day." Patricia reluctantly admitted that was true. Carole also noted that Patricia seemed very reluctant to disappoint the group.

Finally, Patricia talked about being caught between needing to be ready for her in-laws and helping the group. Carole said that Patricia was torn between pleasing her in-laws or the group, but she wondered "What would please Patricia?" The question was followed by more discussion which highlighted Patricia's dilemma. Eventually she said that she would like to help, but it would be better for her if the activity was held some place else. The group agreed to move the party to another location. Bob followed by saying that he had been thinking about Patricia being "put in a bind" trying to please others, and had thought about times when he "got stuck in the same place," and how difficult it was for him. Others in the group readily admitted the same problem and a general discussion ensued about the difficulty of putting your own needs ahead of other.

After some reflection, Patricia became aware of how her thoughts and feelings ("I'm a bad person if I refuse.") led to her acquiescent behavior.

This incident highlights the creation of a successful opportunity for LIA. The leaders focused on highlighting Patricia's dilemma instead of trying to explain its etiology or psychodynamics. It became apparent to Patricia and everyone else what the problem was. Bob's self-disclosure was helpful in promoting universality and inviting others to echo similar feelings.

Summary of Strategies for Facilitating LIA

- Consider novel responses to troublesome patterns.
- Identify participant issues appropriate for LIA.
- Encourage and structure opportunities for LIA.
- Be sensitive to the potentially deficient member.
- Train the group to give feedback.
- Relate the LIA to situations outside the group.
- Keep the issue delimited.

ALTRUISM

"Feeling better through the process of helping another" describes this factor. The helper in some way "extends the self" and experiences satisfaction or perhaps an enhanced self-image as a result of being helpful.

1. Altruistic feelings usually occur when there is encouragement of other important factors, particularly acceptance, universality, guidance, and self-disclosure.

This factor probably develops concurrently with other therapeutic factors. Accepting and supporting another person, indicating how "You are very much like me," via self-disclosure, assisting another to achieve an insight and giving practical information or advice are examples of altruistic actions. Each occurrence offers an opportunity for developing a better feeling about the self. Good feelings that arise from helping usually happen spontaneously and the leader can do little *directly* to create feelings of altruism, other than provide chances for as much positive interaction as possible.

2. Noting when someone has been helpful can assist the development of feelings of altruism.

Many people minimize their helpfulness to others. Occasionally highlighting intermember assistance cannot do any harm and has the potential to be very constructive.

3. Pointing out the secondary consequences as a result of helping has some possibilities for beneficial effects.

It is not only useful to indicate that a person is helpful, but also note what other positive changes may have been evident at the same time. Saying that "You looked really involved and enthusiastic during your exchange with . . ." may help the person experience more fully what it feels like, and how satisfying it can be, to transcend the self.

4. Occasionally structure the group so the helping becomes a natural part of the interaction.

Referring to the earlier case study of Patricia, an alternative strategy may have been for one of the leaders to say "Patricia wants to please her husband's family, but she also wants to please the group. Do you have any feedback on her situation?" This invites members to be helpful in highlighting the dilemma more explicitly or to be more self-disclosing about similar situations from their own lives.

Summary of Strategies for Promoting Altruism

- Prepare people to be helpful during the intake interview.
- High levels of acceptance and universality promote altruism.
- Note when people have been helpful.
- Point out the secondary consequences of helping.
- Create opportunities for helping.

VICARIOUS LEARNING

This type of observational learning occurs either through imitation or the direct association with another member's experience.

Other than modeling effective behavior, there is little the leader can do to promote vicarious learning. Additionally, the literature does not support the efficacy of observational learning experiences for therapy groups. Therefore, there is no compelling reason for the leader to try to create vicarious learning experiences. There are other curative elements which are much more important to develop. If a member identifies with someone's experience in the group, usually it is a spontaneous experience.

1. Promoting universality probably assists with vicarious learning.

If people identify with each other they are more likely to see other people's solutions as fitting themselves. What worked for someone "in the same boat" may well assist them. They may be more willing to attempt a solution that has been effective for another person who appears to have experienced similar problems and situations.

2. Leader modeling of the desired behavior may promote vicarious learning in some circumstances.

There is some limited support for the use of therapist modeling of social skills in short-term, highly structured groups (Bloch & Crouch, 1985). For more complex behavior, the modeling may have no effect, meaning that the participants have not reported imitative behavior an important source of learning.

Summary of Strategies for Promoting Vicarious Learning

- Increase feelings of universality.
- Model desired behavior and specific skills.

SELF-DISCLOSURE

Regardless of how the listener has viewed the incident, when people share material they feel is personal, self-disclosure has taken place.

Self-disclosure is another one of the therapeutic factors which is linked with other components, such as acceptance and feelings of universality. It probably is more efficacious to concentrate on making the group a safe place to disclose, rather than directly promoting self-disclosure.

1. For the majority of people, what they reveal is related to feelings of support and acceptance in the group.

Developing acceptance and universality assists feelings of safety and cohesiveness, and helpful self-disclosures should follow. This therapeutic factor usually is related to the general climate of the group. If the person feels accepted and understood, or feels a sense of kinship with others, self-disclosure will be more likely to follow.

2. Another way of encouraging self-disclosure is for the leader to model it.

There has been little research on leader self-disclosure. One study (Friendlander, Thibodeau, Nichols, Tucker, & Snyder, 1985) investigated the leader's self-disclosing style on outcome measures. With trainee leaders, they found that a low-disclosing leadership style produced more positive outcomes. Corey and Corey (1987) felt the leader's most effective self-disclosures involve reactions to the group process as opposed to the sharing of personal information.

Common-theme groups where the leader shares the same diagnosis as the members usually requires a higher level of disclosure than would be desirable early in a general therapy group. In common-theme groups the members will expect the leader to "show how it is done." Indeed, high levels of disclosure may be part of the mystique of the group. The major role that highly personal revelations play in cancer support groups or drug treatment agencies are obvious examples. There is no evidence that these extensive early confessions necessarily are therapeutic, but many groups have established processes based on tradition rather than evidence.

There is evidence to suggest that early self-disclosure could be misunderstood by clients (Kaul & Bednar, 1986). For example, depending on the type of information divulged, the members may see the leader as unstable or incompetent. How much the leader should reveal, and when, is difficult to determine. Lakin (1985) pointed out that personal self-disclosure, at least temporarily, moves the leader into a member role. This movement represents a role change that the members cannot accomplish. He suggested that leader disclosures evoke very different reactions from those occurring when ordinary members self-disclose. The leader revelations were seen as more valid and potentially more powerful in impact.

In most conditions the best policy is minimal early disclosure of personal information, except for feedback related to the present interactions in the group. The type or depth of self-disclosures can increase as the group becomes more cohesive.

3.   The leader needs to be sensitive about how significant the self-disclosure is for the person.

If the revelation appears important to the person, it should be supported. As is true of acceptance, the leader needs to judge the importance of the self-disclosure, and ensure that the necessary support is forthcoming. When the self-disclosure also involves strong affect, its significance is obvious. More subtle self-disclosures are difficult to read, and their importance to the person can be missed.

4.   Be very aware of how the rest of the group is reacting to a self-disclosure and process reactions which will affect the level of intermember acceptance.

The interface between acceptance and self-disclosure becomes obvious with sensitive self-disclosures. One additional concern is the timing of a self-disclosure. If possible, it is particularly helpful to attempt to keep some types of self-disclosures moderated during the early stages of a group. In some situations the group's reactions to a particular disclosure cannot be ignored.

The following case study illustrates a typical problem which arises from an early intense self-disclosure.

Case Study: Janice

It was the first meeting of a weight control group. The members were discussing some of the reasons they overeat, when Janice suddenly informed them that the major reason she was overeating was due to her physical abuse by her husband. The disclosure produced a stunned and uncomfortable silence.

The leader then expressed her surprise and discomfort and said that "being beaten up seemed like a good reason to overeat to her." She noted that a lot of other people were surprised and uncomfortable also, and asked the rest of the group to share their reactions. After some struggle, and lots of encouragement from the leader, the group was able to verbalize many of the reasons for their anxiety. Members expressed anger at the husband and anger toward Janice for staying with him. They were worried whether they were expected to disclose details about their current or past family. The leader had to expend a substantial amount of time and energy to give Janice the support she needed and address the anger and fear of the other women.

What the leader *did not pursue* was a discussion of Janice's relationship with her husband. In her view, extensive discussion of the participants' outside relationships was not part of the contract for the group. She thought that to take on such a difficult problem in the group would not only frighten some of the other women (which it had), but would be a serious departure from the reason for the group's existence. The members had contracted for a common-theme group designed to help them develop effective weight control methods.

The intervention illustrated an occasion when a leader's self-disclosure invites other members to participate. The leader processed reactions to Janice instead of discussing Janice's marriage, which was more productive for the group.

5. Clarify the *type* of self-disclosures which are appropriate for the group.

The case example illustrates how some types of disclosures are not appropriate for some groups. The best place to discuss what is and is not suitable material for the planned group, is during the intake interview (see Chapter 2).

If a group leader chooses to pursue every issue the members might disclose, the group contract is violated. It may be essential at times to handle some individual concerns outside the group. With the example of Janice, the leader could have said, "You certainly have some concerns, but we can't really deal with your marriage in this group. Could you see me for a few minutes when we finish here, and I will try to give you some ideas about what you might do." The external meeting allows the leader to show support and explain more about why the group was not the right place for her to talk about her abuse.

Summary of Strategies with Self-Disclosure

- Increased acceptance facilitates self-disclosure.
- Model self-disclosure primarily by process statements.
- Be alert for covert communications.
- Be aware of how the group is reacting to a disclosure.
- Ensure proper support for important self-disclosures.
- Plan what types of disclosures are appropriate.

INSIGHT (SELF-UNDERSTANDING)

Insight relates to learning something new and important about the self. The self-understanding may relate to the etiology of the problem, or a clearer comprehension about the nature of the difficulty, or may involve some new perception based on feedback received in the group.

As might be expected, the leader's particular theoretical orientation becomes important for insight to occur. Which therapeutic model offers better opportunities for insight is unknown. In fact there is almost no research that appropriately compares one form of group intervention with another. The only extensive study of comparative approaches (Lieberman et al., 1973) found no superiority for any one system and any differences of outcome related to clusters of leader behavior regardless of the theoretical system they employed.

It is likely that outcomes for group approaches will emulate the results from individual forms of intervention. Individual therapies show an advantage for cognitive or behavior therapies (and mixtures of the two) for some types of specific disorders. The superiority of these systems has not been decisive for all problems. It is likely that nonspecific factors, such as client type or therapist style, provide the best overall explanation for positive results (Lambert, Sharpiro, & Bergin, 1986). However, there are some guidelines which are helpful.

1. Each leader needs a clear practical model to communicate to the participant.

The model should offer an explanation for the etiology of problems and suggest guidelines for future change. A leader probably could offer an existential, psychoanalytic, or behavioral explanation for a particular problem, and precipitate change in the person, as long as the client believes "it." If the leader believes the offered insight makes sense and communicates that belief to the client, it may be enough to create the possibility of insight. As Bloch and Crouch (1985, p. 44) proposed, "What is crucial is an understanding by the patient, shared by his therapist, which makes sense and leads to a reduction in the patient's state of bewilderment."

The chosen model needs to be one that can be communicated clearly and quickly to the individual, and applicable for a wide variety of experiences. The theoretical representation is not only useful for explaining the current responses of the person, but can be utilized to indicate how behavior may be different in the future. Clear and comprehensive models can be learned, adopted, and used by the participants inside and outside the group.

Another argument for practical, simple systems in groups is that there can be effective member to member feedback. The more the group members understand a particular model, the greater the probability they will use it with each other.

2. The chosen model should provide a mechanism for linking thoughts, feelings, and behavior.

This contention has not been tested conclusively. If the feedback to a group member includes all three components, that is, thoughts, feelings, and behavior, then there is a greater opportunity for change. For instance, "When you *feel* angry it seems you are *thinking* . . . , and then you tend to *act* . . ." provides the person with clear links and allows more opportunities for change. Previously cited research strongly endorsed linking cognitions with any affective experience. There is additional gain possible by insuring that the recipient understands how the behavior connects with thoughts and feelings.

In some cases a system is invented for a particular group, particularly a common-theme group. For example, one leader developed the acronym CAT for stress management groups. First, it is harder to imagine anything that usually looks more relaxed (or stressed) at times, so the model has good associative value.

Second, the CAT (Cue-Activity-Talk) refers to a system for analyzing physiological reactions, thoughts, feelings and behavior. The members easily learned to apply it to themselves or to each other when faced with stressful circumstances.

3.   Describe behavior rather than labelling or making interpretations about people.

Careful observation can be an effective way to provide numerous possibilities for insight without referring to a model of any kind. Simply noting and communicating to the person what you noted may be effective in many situations. An observation such as, "I noticed that when several members of the group said how well you were doing, you looked uncomfortable and then immediately changed the topic," can be the first step in new self-understanding. The feedback makes the person aware of how they behaved when praised and offers them the opportunity to evaluate associated thoughts and feelings.

4.   If possible, give the person options for changes in thoughts feelings or behavior.

Another persuasive reason for including all three components in a model is that it gives the client more options for effective action, depending on the person's particular style. Some people are more comfortable considering changes to their behavior, others work more effectively with feelings, and many find examining and changing their thoughts or imagery more effective. If a feedback/change model is restricted to one modality, there are limited options for both insight and change.

Case Study: Ellen

Ellen was a recent addition to a group in an outpatient facility. This particular group included eight men and women who were spouses of alcoholics. Tim led the group, and he was not very experienced with leadership. Each group meeting followed a large group lecture about some concern pertinent to the spouses. This was the third time Ellen had attended the meetings. On the two previous occasions she had started the sessions expressing anger about the preceding lecture and the group in general. The leader had allowed the anger to continue both occasions. The first time the leader thought (hoped) that maybe the person just needed to unwind. When Ellen continued her tirade during the second meeting the leader became concerned as she was dominating the group and controlling most of the interaction.

Prior to the third meeting of the group Tim consulted with his colleagues about how to handle Ellen if her behavior continued. As suspected Ellen began the meeting as she had the other two, expressing her disgust about the "stupid lecture" and stated that her husband was the problem (not her) and further indicated that the "group was probably going to be another wasted evening." At this point Tim said directly to Ellen that he was "feeling very uncomfortable with her, wanted to be able to relate to her but did not know how to get past her anger." She responded with more anger and said that if he had to live like she did, he would be angry too. Tim replied with a statement that he was so uncomfortable with her anger that he was having trouble hearing anything else. Ellen continued her tirade and Tim, very firmly, asked her to stop for a minute. He then pointed out her pattern over the last three weeks. She came to the group angry, and any attempt on his part, or anyone else's, to make contact with her was strongly rejected. He said that he felt she must feel really alone and that he would like to be helpful, but he needed her to tell him what to do and how the group might help. Ellen responded with anger, although with reduced intensity, and looked teary. Tim stated that a year ago when his wife continually refused to get help he felt totally alone and helpless and he wondered if Ellen might be feeling the same. She started to bluster again, but one of the group members said that he thought Ellen was scared and that he understood that. He was scared a lot too.

This intervention appeared to defuse Ellen considerably and she began to cry, yet still sounded angry when she talked. The anger gradually left her as she began to discuss her family and its problems and her inability to make things any better. During the rest of the session, the leader and the rest of the group tried to help Ellen understand her pattern of behavior. Eventually she could see that she denied her fear because she saw it as a weakness. The anger helped Ellen hide the fear, which was a manifestation of the self-loathing she felt for her lack of coping. So when she really wanted help ("felt weak" in her system), her aggressive behavior had the effect of driving people away even more, which meant she felt more alone, needy, and powerless.

Ellen was able to see the self-defeating pattern of what she was doing and how her thoughts and behavior perpetuated her negative view of self. When no one helped, she felt justified in behaving like an angry person. The anger prevented her getting the understanding and support she so badly needed.

Situations where one person negatively dominates the group manner are difficult to handle. At the same time, such occurrences provide excellent opportunities for insight, and it is worthwhile to pursue the problem situation. Additionally, there is no better confidence-booster than tackling someone like Ellen and having some success. Tim used a very sound opening strategy, that is, he expressed his reactions without blaming Ellen. He continued that tactic and repeated it as needed. Additionally, Tim tried to focus Ellen on what she wanted. As required however, he had no hesitation to ask Ellen to "stop for a minute." Sometimes, a time out from the troublesome behavior is necessary to start a reflective process.

The supporting intervention from another group member was extremely helpful in this case, but a leader cannot depend on the group's assistance. Without support, Tim's approach would have continued as before until he could make some kind of positive contact with Ellen.

Summary of Strategies for Assisting Insight

- Develop a clear model to use in interventions.
- Link thoughts, feelings, and behavior.
- Make observations rather than interpretations.
- In difficult situations, analyze the context of the behavior.
- State how you are reacting to difficult behavior.
- Give options for change when possible.

CATHARSIS

The process of catharsis involves some type of affective release. As a consequence of the emotional expression there is a feeling of relief. Attaching cognitive structure to the expression of feeling is helpful.

In strictest terms, the operation of this therapeutic factor does not require any type of response from the rest of the group. The feeling of relief is enough in some cases to cause positive change. If the catharsis involves a sensitive self-disclosure, then the leader needs to ensure that the person feels supported.

1. Allow a cathartic experience to occur naturally rather than attempting to promote it.

One of the key issues associated with catharsis is the controversy about whether a leader should encourage or provoke cathartic experiences. Although in some situations the group members may report short-term benefits from intense emotional experiences, the long-term consequences may not be positive, particularly when the feeling expressed is anger. Also, there is clear evidence that leaders who emphasize emotional stimulation in the group are more likely to have casualties. Some people have been significantly damaged by extreme catharsis in the group experience (Lieberman et al., 1973). Encouraging participants to "let it all hang out" is not only not helpful, but also psychologically dangerous. There is no compelling reason for the leader deliberately to try to create a cathartic experience. Unfortunately, some individuals expect catharsis to be a prerequisite for change. If they fail to have a strong affective release during a group, it means they have not really benefited from the experience.

2. Place the cathartic experience in a clearly understandable frame of reference.

Most theorists feel leaders who emphasize cognitive and reflective experiences show more positive changes in their groups (for example, Corey & Corey, 1987). The leader can use a cathartic experience to create meaning for the person, and a model for understanding and change is linked to the experience following the incident. Leaders probably gain more from emphasizing behaviors associated with universality, acceptance, and insight rather than facilitating a cathartic experience.

Case Study: Sarah

A group of five women and three men were in the third session of a personal growth group. The leader, Alice, was very experienced and felt that the group had been unusually accepting and supportive in the few sessions. Midway through the session the interaction focused on some uneasiness between one of the young women (Sarah) and the oldest male (Bryan) in the group. Sarah reported feeling very anxious when Bryan talked to her but did not know why. He was puzzled by her reaction, said he liked her a lot so far, and didn't know what to make of Sarah's reaction. After more exploration, Sarah became very tearful and extremely anxious, which rapidly progressed to semi-hysteria. Some of the other women comforted Sarah, and Alice chose to let her "cry it out" until she became calm enough to consider her strong reactions.

After Sarah had calmed down, Alice asked if she was willing to talk about her reactions or whether she wanted to "let it be" for now. Sarah said that her reactions were connected to a time when her stepfather sexually abused her. She was still very tearful and upset at this point and said she did not want to talk any more right now. The leader supported her decision not to pursue the issue, and said that she hoped Sarah would talk about her feelings later in this meeting or another meeting, but only when she felt like it. Then the leader briefly reaffirmed a person's right "not to talk." Alice indicated that, although some people might want to discuss their reactions right now, they needed to respect Sarah's wishes. She told Bryan that she knew he must have a lot of feelings right now, but that surely he realized that Sarah's reactions had nothing to do with him. Finally, Alice moved the discussion to another topic.

3. Protect the member who has an intense emotional experience.

The first time that a group experiences a strong affective reaction from one of its members, the leader's responses will set precedents for future episodes. Consider the example of Sarah: first, the cathartic experience developed naturally; Second, the leader supported and protected Sarah during and after the incident; Third, the rest of the group observed a process which increased their sense of personal safety. The leader demonstrated clearly that a member in distress will be supported and given as much control of the process as possible. Some group members were left with unresolved feelings about the episode, yet Alice could not allow the rest of the group to discuss their reactions to what had occurred until Sarah could participate. Sarah did not choose to pursue the topic any further and the leader was obligated to support that choice.

Finally, Alice attempted to offer Bryan some support before moving on and reaffirmed his lack of responsibility for Sarah's feelings. In this case there was information which allowed the leader to separate Bryan personally from Sarah's distress. In other situations, where the strong reaction might be more of a result of current relationships, it may be harder for the leader to handle the "other person."

Summary of Strategies Associated with Catharsis

- Allow cathartic experience to occur naturally.
- Protect the person having the experience.
- End the experience cleanly when it is time to move on.
- Process reactions to the experience when possible.

GUIDANCE

Two primary activities illustrate guidance functions. First, there is the simple imparting of information. Second, there is the process of giving advice or suggestions.

In comparison to other therapeutic factors, guidance activities require little elaboration. What type and how much information should be offered is a function of the type of group. Although research with traditional psychotherapy groups does not support the use of guidance, there are some studies which have reported its effectiveness (for example, Andrews, 1991; Stern et al., 1984). Providing accurate and timely information are important activity when there are health considerations. Suggestions for coping techniques can also be beneficial. It is unlikely however, that direct advice about an individual's life would have the same value. Most practitioners agree that statements which carry the "What you should do is ..." imperative are fraught with negative possibilities.

Another implicit message in advice is the inference that the person's solutions have the potential for being unsatisfactory or that they do not need to take responsibility for their own actions. Suggesting a strategy is a viable form of advice. Directing the person to leave a spouse, get a new job, or take a vacation has little value. The outcome for advice-giving often results in the recipient returning to say, "Well I tried what you said and it didn't work!"

1. Make sure the offered information is accurate.

This suggestion is basic, yet some group leaders get into trouble because they had not bothered to check some old information. Particularly with medical problems, leaders need to be sure that what they tell people is current and accurate.

2. Do not assume people have basic information.

Psychologists who work in medical settings have considerable experience with people who do not know the basics about a condition. Even if patients previously have talked to a medical specialist, the family physician and several allied health personnel, they still may not know the "facts." In reality, they may have been told, but they still do not *know*. In many circumstances they were not told, or the information was not conveyed clearly, or they did not understand what was said.

3. If at all possible make the learning active rather than passive.

Integrate knowing and doing together. Brief mini-lectures in a group probably will not do much harm, but long didactic presentations usually fail to involve the participants. Think of active ways for the participants to gain knowledge. For example, instead of telling a group of people with diabetes about the different symptoms which might be attributable to the disease, have the members volunteer their own reactions. The group generates a checklist of possible symptoms, which leads to a discussion about suggested coping techniques for each symptom.

Summary of Guidance Activities

- Give direct advice sparingly.
- Ensure that people have applicable information.

- Verify that information is current and accurate.
- Make learning active.

HOPE

The belief that life can be better, that one can change personal reactions, or change circumstances is the cornerstone of therapy, whether offered individually or in groups. In general, increasing optimism about the future is therapeutic in itself.

The intake interview is the first opportunity to begin to increase feelings of hope. Once the group begins, the leader can encourage the development of optimism. As other factors develop, it is likely feelings of hope will increase concomitantly. An increased sense of acceptance, universality, insight, or episodes of LIA offer possibilities for effecting hope, and almost any positive experience can be helpful (Couch & Childers, 1987).

1.   Note positive changes in members as they occur.

Saying, "You seem to be much more involved in trying to reduce your level of medication," highlights a member's positive movement. As is true in many other interactions, the leader can stay alert as to how members are reacting to successes as well as to problem situations.

2.   Make sure members are aware when positive and hopeful themes are part of the process.

Many times a group moves from recounting past failures to an enthusiastic recitation of successes and positive expectations. Any movement toward positive discussions can be noted and highlighted by the leader. The leader is in a position to more readily observe the constructive movement and to make the participants aware of it.

3.   Make the positive review process part of the group design.

Many treatment programs have formal public "graduation ceremonies" designed to reinforce those graduating and serve as reminders for others still in the program that they can succeed. Common-theme groups frequently have progress checks as part of the ongoing process, which provides occasions to reinforce success. Structuring time for people to report their new insights or attempts at new ways of behaving, can enhance the development of hope.

Summary of Strategies for Promoting Hope

- Point out participant successes as they occur.
- Note positive themes in the group.
- Build positive reviews into the group design.

GENERAL STRATEGIES WITH THE THERAPEUTIC FACTORS

In general, the development of most therapeutic factors are associated with positive outcomes. Promoting a high level of acceptance and universality is important for the well-being of the members, and for preventing negative outcomes. These two primary factors are functionally related to what many theorists refer to as "cohesiveness." It is likely that as feelings of acceptance and universality increase, meaningful self-disclosures will occur, which will augment the working atmosphere of the group. Leaders may use the type and frequency of self-disclosures as a barometer of the group mood.

As is true of any type of therapy, insight is an important cause of positive change. Attaining self-understanding is largely theory specific, and the type of insight sought depends upon the objectives of the group. Self-understanding is facilitated by offering a clear model to the participants.

LIA is one of the therapeutic factors unique to groups and many participants report it to be a main source of new learning. Learning from interpersonal actions is well worth emphasizing, although the relative emphasis on LIA depends upon the type of group.

There is little the leader can do to create vicarious learning. This factor seems to be dependent upon the relatively spontaneous identification process that one person has in response to another's work in the group. Even if it occurs, participants have not reported vicarious learning to be an important source of learning.

To a large degree, altruistic acts occur spontaneously. The leader may remind members that they can help, and reinforce them when they do help. Nonetheless, increased feelings of self-worth or personal satisfaction as a consequence of helping another is difficult to influence directly. Fostering support and acceptance in the group increases the opportunities for altruism to occur.

Leaders can encourage catharsis gently through the use of support and feedback, but should not provoke it due to the dangers of negative outcomes. Once it occurs, the leader's main task is to ensure the safety of the individual. Later, it is helpful to attach meaning and a cognitive structure to the experience.

Finally, other than being positive and optimistic (which should not be underestimated), increased feelings of hope parallel the development of many of the other curative elements. The members will be more optimistic when they feel support, realize others have similar feelings, gain insight, or demonstrate change in a variety of other ways.

6

EVALUATING GROUPS IN PROGRESS

The initial development and design of a group entails a considerable amount of thought and planning. Unfortunately, the careful consideration of strategies does not end once the group has started. Many a group leader has discovered that, despite careful initial planning and selection of members, the group evolved in an entirely unexpected direction. At times, leading a group requires a continual process of analysis and modification. Even if the group is going smoothly, its process needs to be assessed periodically. There are several models and processes which can be used in the critique, analysis, and modification of a group in progress.

THE NEED FOR CONTINUING EVALUATION

Groups are both intriguing and frustrating because of their unpredictability. What was planned may, or may not, happen. What seemed to be a great idea at the time falls flat when it is implemented. Careful evaluation of progress *during* the group is essential. Once the group is underway there is a need to monitor its development throughout, from the first session to a post-group follow-up. Monitoring the continuing process of the individual's and group's evolution can be demanding, but the payoff in a well-conducted process makes the expenditure of energy worthwhile.

Moreover, most leaders find it essential to know what they are doing and the effects it has. There is certainly a danger in *assuming* the effects of a group process.

> *They rely mainly upon clinical judgement to assess the effects of group therapy, . . . evidence indicates that clinicians are often insensitive to group process and client change (Dies and Teleska 1985, p. 138).*

In their review of the negative effects of group psychotherapy, the authors suggested that many leaders underestimate the powerful impact of group dynamics. They urged more systematic and objective evaluations of groups to protect participants from negative outcomes.

Many psychologists have been concerned with the impact of intense group experiences. The possibility of negative effects was confirmed in a study of encounter groups (Lieberman et al., 1973). The leaders, although they were highly experienced, were alarmingly ineffective in identifying people in their group who were damaged by the process. Of the 16 clearly identified casualties which resulted from the groups, the leaders correctly identified only two possibilities. In contrast, the participants could correctly name 12 of the 16 members who were hurt by the experience.

Similar results were obtained (Hausman, 1979; p. 194) in a study of two groups for parents of children who were attending a guidance clinic. The leaders failed to understand ". . . what each individual perceived or valued about the complex group experience." In addition, the leaders showed substantial disagreement with the members about what factors were helpful.

More recent evidence has not been any more encouraging. A study which investigated a process for measuring cohesion in group psychotherapy used extensive observer ratings to observe video segments of groups. The ratings and outcome measures proved to be reliable, but the researchers concluded:

> *It was somewhat perplexing to find that the observer ratings of cohesion correlate highly with patient-rated outcomes and not with therapists' ratings of outcome. Other data available to us indicate that patients' ratings of benefit in*

this study correlated highly with improvements on a variety of symptom measures. Therapist ratings of benefit, on the other hand, had no such relationship (Budman et al., 1987; p. 87).

In this research, the group leaders were not able to identify which of the participants actually benefited from the experience. Conversely, when individuals in the group reported progress it was verified by independent measures. One important consideration in these studies was the use of independent, uninvolved observers or independent ratings to determine who had a negative or positive outcome.

A related study compared therapist and client perceptions of curative factors. There was a marked inconsistency between the two groups of ratings in what each group perceived as helpful. Of most concern was the tendency for therapists to see ". . . growth where the clients felt pain." (Bonney, Randell, & Cleveland, 1986; p. 318). Only one client from the entire group agreed with the therapist on the helpfulness of the experience.

Finally, a small sample study (Hobbs, Birtchnell, Harte, & Lacey, 1989) of women with bulimia showed the same type of disagreement. Leaders and members were asked to use the *Most Important Event* questionnaire following each session in an attempt to determine which therapeutic factor had the most impact. The participants responses were compared with the two treating therapists, and there was agreement on only 5 of the 30 ratings.

Although there are relatively few studies that directly compared the perceptions of the leader and the participants, they all suggest a danger when leaders assume their perceptions of the member's experience is accurate. One way of avoiding the whole problem is to gather objective information systematically about the experiences of the participants.

Ethical concerns are also germane to this issue. A fitting analogy might involve a situation where a physician has prescribed a drug which has potential severe negative side effects. The hypothetical physician knows a routine procedure that indicates when harm is being done by the medication. If the doctor fails to perform the routine testing and the patient is injured, then due professional care has not been exercised. There is a strong argument for employing brief questionnaires, or a similar device, to supplement a leader's perceptions of the progress of the individuals in the group.

THE CONTINUING EVALUATION PROCESS

In addition to monitoring the members' reactions to the process, repeated assessment offers opportunities to gather information that is helpful for making alterations to the group design. Another use of the periodic evaluation is to provide useful research data. The clinical situation provides repeated opportunities to refine evaluation devices and trial different methodologies. All of these purposes may be accomplished without seriously interfering with the operation of a group, or significantly increasing the work load of the therapists.

The following comprises the major components that may be included in the routine group evaluation.

1. Leader(s) postsession consultation which includes a critique of the:

   a. current state of the leader(s).
   b. general process of the group.
   c. important positive or negative incidents.
   d. personal and interpersonal characteristics of each member.

2. Postsession input from the participants which includes:

   a. feedback related to the objectives of the group.
   b. participants' ratings on the therapeutic factors and other concerns related to process.

The first half of the evaluation is performed in the session critique by the coleaders, or possibly in a consultation meeting when the group is conducted by one leader. Usually, the feedback from the participants is gathered at the end of a session with a questionnaire. There is no need for an extensive or time consuming procedure to conduct the evaluation. With a clear and comprehensive design, a one-page form, which normally takes about two minutes to complete, can gather the needed information.

LEADER'S CONSULTATION

Leading groups can be exhausting as well as exhilarating. Whether the session was a good or bad experience, it is useful to take the time to handle one's own feelings about the experience before the group analysis begins. The reconciliation of the leader's feelings creates a more positive atmosphere for analysis and problem solving. More importantly, the postgroup consultation is a major way for the leadership to take care of personal issues and avoid burnout. Even when there is only one leader, and the supervision is scheduled some time after the group, the reconciliation process is helpful.

Coleaders need to meet as soon as possible after the session to clear any problems between them, and continue the relationship maintenance necessary to work effectively together. It is important for the coleaders to work on their relationship and to discuss situations where they have unresolved feelings about each other's behavior. Circumstances where one leader felt annoyed with the other are particularly important to work through. Also, other potential difficulties, such as confusion about the process or objectives need to be resolved. Very minor incidents, if unresolved, can accumulate and create tension between the leaders, which can be communicated to the group.

The postgroup process is also a time for mutual support and encouragement, and the maintenance of a positive relationship. Part of the consultation involves giving each other feedback, or obtaining input from a colleague/supervisor. An examination of effective and ineffective leadership performance forms part of the review, as well as considerations of how to improve. The postgroup consultation is critical for the leader's development and the successful progress toward meeting the participant's needs.

GENERAL PROCESS CRITIQUE

Following the leader's critique, the next step is a review of the overall process of the group in the session. This part of the analysis can be expedited by carefully recalling what the group actually did from the beginning to the closing. As each step is recalled, inferences can be made about the meaning and effect of the series of events. Alternatively, some leaders like to re-examine the entire process of the group before doing any analysis. In either case, the analysis includes an objective recall of the events, followed by a subjective appraisal of meaning and effect of the events. Naturally, the subjective evaluation would be influenced by the theoretical orientation of the leadership. At the end of this process an overall picture of how the group as a whole is behaving should emerge. This analysis makes it possible to develop future strategies for moving the group and individuals toward the stated goals.

A useful framework for analysis is provided by group developmental theory. Certain types of interpersonal behavior are often associated with a particular stage of development. Frequently, stages in the group involve the attempted resolution of interpersonal issues, and the degree of movement in a group can often be judged by the types of concerns prevalent in the interaction. Following are some examples of stages, developmental issues, and general leadership strategies.

GROUP ISSUES AND STAGES
OF DEVELOPMENT

Beginning Stage

At this stage members struggle to be included in the group. The predominant concern is one of being liked, and issues of acceptance and universality are foremost in the process.

Member Behavior

Minimal self-disclosures
Reliance on the leadership
Subtle testing of the leadership
Avoidance of negative feedback
Emphasis on consensus
Frequent advice or suggestions
Active search for commonalities
Avoidance of conflict

Leader Strategies

The best way to resolve the beginning work of the group is to focus on increasing the levels of interpersonal acceptance and universality. Stated differently, the leader attempts to develop cohesion in the group. Simple structured exercises that allow contact in smaller groups are often helpful. Process comments that highlight inclusion themes and actions may be useful. Leaders have to balance teaching the group how to work effectively without exerting too much control of the process.

Awareness Stage

Issues of inclusion are still important, but self-control and interpersonal control are more essential. Foremost is a concern about how much one has to give up to be included and gain from the group.

Member Behavior

Risky self-disclosures increase
Meaningful personal feedback begins
Conflict is allowed
Active support intensifies
Ambivalence about the group is verbalized
Testing of who has the influence in the group
Trust issues arise
Leadership is openly tested
Operating rules are negotiated
Alliances are formed

Leader Strategies

The leader can begin to develop learning from interpersonal actions (LIA) by modeling and teaching feedback models. Altruistic acts are encouraged, and the group will be encouraged to conduct their own work as much as possible. Conflicts are worked through as they arise, and the leader will have to ensure that substantial support is available. The most rigorous challenges to the leaders occur during this stage, and it may be difficult at times to handle disputes nondefensively.

Working Stage

Reciprocal sharing and support become established in the group. Members are concerned about being helped, and being helpful.

Member Behavior

Mutual support shown
Intimacy attempted
Conflict is accepted rather than avoided

Self-responsibility is stressed
Personal independence is established
Altruism becomes evident
Active work on insight and LIA take place
Hopeful statements increase

Leader Strategies

This stage is the most enjoyable part of a group. Members have learned about the process, how to conduct the group, and to take a lot more responsibility for themselves. Leaders can be actively supportive, make group theme and process comments, and confront members if necessary. One common obstacle during this stage is that members sometimes are reluctant to overtly negotiate changes in norms and operating procedures as they occur. New rules or ways of operating may emerge without any testing of consensus by the members. The leader may need to directly intervene in the process in order to avoid fragmentation within the group.

Ending Stage

Concerns with separation, and sometimes grief, are common. The major theme revolves around issues of independence versus dependence.

Member Behavior

Intimate relationships emphasized
Conflict minimized
Abandonment themes surface in discussion
Group termination is resisted
Optimistic statements about the future are frequent
Anxiety is expressed about coping alone

Leader Strategies

Other than the usual process tasks which were employed earlier in the group, the leader's main efforts will be directed toward focusing the issues of termination and independence. The members may need to be reminded frequently that the group *will* end, and participants will be left to their own devices. If appropriate for the group, relapse prevention may be part of the termination process.

Analysis of the major forms of interpersonal behavior would allow the leaders to have a good idea of what developmental stage the group has reached. Awareness of the primary issues makes it possible for the leaders to develop strategies for handling the concerns within each stage.

Individual Analysis

As the group continues, an individual analysis of each member is recommended as part of the postgroup analysis. First, what personal concerns has the *individual* expressed? These types of concerns often refer to feelings and thoughts that reflect a poor self-image, chronic anxiety or depression, or the tendency to be self-critical. Additional examples include current life stressors, such as a recent divorce, or loss of employment. These difficulties are unique to the person and exist outside the group.

Second, what are the prevailing interpersonal issues in the current group? These problems may be feelings of noninvolvement in the process, or concerns about being rejected by the other people, or feeling hurt and angry about an incident that has occurred in the group. The interpersonal and personal issues may be highly interdependent. An individual who has a poor self-image may fear rejection, which produces cautious, or passive, group behavior. If the intrapersonal issues are reflected in interpersonal behavior, they may be linked in the group, which creates more opportunities for LIA or insight. If the personal concern is not related to an individual's group behavior, the leaders can still be alert for the possibility that the person's reactions may be exacerbated by the life stressor.

The person-by-person inventory could include ideas about the individual's strengths, interpersonal style, and what alliances have been formed with other members. Another benefit of the participant inventory is that the leader can become more aware of limited information about someone. This may be due to infrequent participation, or it may be due to the leader's lack of attention to the person. In the latter case, there is a need for consultation to discover why the person has been largely ignored and possible countertransference reactions can be examined, and hopefully, rectified. This process allows leaders to examine any interpersonal distortions that might prevent understanding and active support of the person. Finally, an additional benefit of the personal inventory is that the leader may become more aware of themes that are common to a number of participants. The identified theme can be developed in the group to increase feelings of universality.

Interpersonal Analysis

Leaders need to know what types of personal relationship are currently manifested in the group. Each member is evaluated in terms of relative closeness with others. Bonding with others, as well as evidence of distance or conflict, is evaluated and noted. The leader becomes more mindful of subgroups that may be a problem, or isolates who are potential casualties. Overall, this procedure would provide data about the development of cohesion in the group, suggest issues that are being avoided, and provide valuable information for planning.

Further, the interpersonal inventory can provide ideas about how to proceed. If subgroups are identified, they may be diffused by exercises which allow more interpersonal contact and bonding. Again, in the case of a person who appears to be isolated from the group, the analysis may identify someone who has similar issues, and contact between the two may be facilitated.

An evaluation of the level of interpersonal acceptance assists with future planning. Many "neutral" relationships may signal that the leaders are being too controlling and the members are not being allowed to interact sufficiently. Identification of antagonistic interactions signals a need to use more time to process and resolve conflict.

At times simply placing the identified problems on the group "agenda" is an effective solution. In general therapy groups, the problems are easier to address because the members often have clearer expectations that they are to learn from each other's interpersonal behavior. In common-theme groups, some of the identified concerns may be handled more appropriately through designed exercises or procedures. Additionally, common-theme groups are more likely to be time-restricted, and the leader has to balance the interpersonal process needs with the requirements of gaining requisite knowledge, information, and skills.

Group Problems

There are times when the personal or interpersonal evaluation indicates patterns which are impeding the group's development. One way of approaching troublesome patterns is to assume that the behaviors reflect a transaction which is designed to produce predictable consequences. The inquiry asks three questions regarding the problem situation:

1. What are the behaviors? As objectively as possible, what actually occurred?

2. What are the actions designed to do? Detail the behavioral consequences of the group or the individual.

3. What does it mean? Generate hypotheses about *why* the event has occurred.

The purpose of the analysis is to help the leader identify a pattern to the actions, so that a strategy to alter it may be initiated.

Warm Up

A group of eight people has been together for five weeks in a personal growth group. For the past three weeks the leader, who prefers to make minimal interventions in the group, notices that the group begins with a 10–15 minute discussion which is rather social and superficial. This period of discussion appears to act as a "warm up" and the group gradually then moves into its work for the day.

In this case the behavior is the group's 10–15 minutes of social interchange. The consequence of the behavior is that the general level of anxiety in the group is reduced, which allows more productive work to occur. The next step examines what the group behavior means. Although there could be several plausible explanations, a common meaning of such behavior is there is initial anxiety in the group due to reasons such as: (1) The members are still ambivalent about the group; and (2) they do not have the skills to know how to move directly into more intimate contact. The social exchanges allow the members to "make contact," and thus reduce anxiety, before more serious work begins.

How the leader chooses to deal with the behavior is dependent on the type of group, and the objectives for the session. For example, in a general therapy group the leader might simply point out the group's behavior and ask the members to reflect on how they feel and act when the group begins. In a short-term common-theme group, the leader might choose to design an intervention which changed the way the group opened so the members could learn to make contact in a more productive way.

The same process can be applied to an individual's problem behavior.

A Late Issue

A group for single parents was in its tenth session. About ten minutes before the scheduled end of the group a member raised a difficult personal issue and requested feedback from the group about it. The concern could obviously not be handled in the remaining time. This was the second time the member had waited till the last minute to ask for assistance. The group responded with a lot of frustration and annoyance, and the member felt hurt and rejected by the group reaction.

Participants raising sensitive issues late in the group is not an uncommon problem. In this situation the behavior had two consequences, frustration and annoyance by the group, and feelings of rejection by the individual. Several hunches are possible about what the pattern means, but two are: (1) The member is testing his acceptance level in the group. In other words, do they like me enough to stay late to help me? (2) The person is already angry or disappointed with the group and wants to verify its lack of value. At a minimum, the leader can simply highlight what has happened and suggest the group analyze the transaction during the next meeting.

The behavior-consequences-meaning process can be applied to almost any situation, and if nothing else, can provide some hypotheses about troublesome individual or group behavior. Obviously, there is an assumption associated with this type of analysis. There is the belief that many of the actions have been specifically motivated, consciously or unconsciously, to produce known consequences which are part of a pattern of reciprocal interpersonal operations. Put more simply, people frequently act in ways which have known "payoffs." These actions represent repeated patterns of behavior which can sometimes be illuminated within the group process.

GROUP THEMES

Another perspective on groups has been offered by the idea that groups have common conflicts, or themes which significantly affect the dynamics of the interactions. These subjects become the dominant force in the interpersonal relationships and the interactions of the entire group. In its purest form, the leader who accepts this point of view might not make any individual interventions, but simply address the group as a whole when, for example, describing feelings of anxiety. In other words, it is not the individual's anxiety which is the problem, the feeling is only a manifestation of the groups' anxiety. Some theorists have modified this stance and advocated that the leader address individual concerns first before tackling a group theme (Horwitz, 1989).

It is likely that these 'group as a whole' types of interventions would not be readily understood, or valued, in many short-term common-theme groups. However, the idea that groups have shared themes can be useful for the leader during the analysis of a current group. It is useful to review the group in terms of what kinds of recurring issues have been the focus of discussion the interaction. Whitaker (1985, p. 35) has suggested:

> *A shared theme is an issue or a concern which comes to preoccupy a group and dominate the attention of the members for a period of time. A theme has affect attached to it but also has content: a theme is about something. Not unusual group themes have to do with a sense of being bad, or a sense of being a victim of injustice, or a yearning for a quick magical solution to one's problems.*

In a thematic review, the leaders try to evaluate the verbal and non-verbal content to determine what meanings are being addressed at a covert (dynamic) level. Once the theme has been identified, leaders will become more aware of the current needs of the group and can look for opportunities to make the concerns more of an overt part of the interaction. Even in a short-term group, there is much the leaders can do to assist the participants in handling such thoughts and feelings.

INPUT FROM PARTICIPANTS

In addition to the postgroup evaluation by the leaders, there needs to be a routine evaluation by the members. Ideally, part of the weekly or biweekly evaluation by participants consists of feedback on: (1) progress toward contracted goals in the group, and (2) the client's perception of the dynamic or therapeutic factors associated with the process. A one-page checklist or set of simple scales can be used to obtain the needed information. The leader may choose to gather the information anonymously and ask the members to place the completed form in a "mailbox" as they leave. The anonymous approach is appropriate for some type of research efforts. Some practitioners might see the anonymous evaluation process as inviting a lack of honesty by the group members and eventually impeding the development of cohesion. They would prefer clients to confront their concerns directly in the group. On the other hand, some participants are not ready to voice their fears directly to the group. In a brief common-theme group, the lack of time or opportunities to do so, may prevent using the group to resolve issues with acceptance or universality. Ultimately, the preferred option is for the group to decide whether the feedback is to be anonymous or not. Anonymous feedback is preferable to no feedback at all. Research cited earlier in this chapter strongly suggests there is a danger in the leaders relying solely on their own perceptions of how members are reacting to the group process. There seems to be no reasonable justification for risking a negative outcome with a person. Additionally, the participant feedback allows for more precise planning of the group experience.

Contract Evaluation

Monitoring the individual's improvement as the group continues is both necessary and helpful. Without such information therapeutic failures can result that could have been prevented by a very simple adjustment to the process, or a slight change in emphasis. An additional reason for a continuing evaluation is that it demonstrates to the members that the leadership is concerned about their progress. Also, the survey helps people focus on their own changes, or lack of changes. At its most simple level, asking the person about their progress toward a contracted goal is effective. For instance, simple questions like the following can provide useful information.

1.   I am making good progress toward what I want to accomplish in this group.

Strongly Agree	Agree	?	Disagree	Strongly Disagree

2. What could the group do to help you make more progress?

Where specific training is being offered as part of the group, relative skill acquisition can also be evaluated in much the same way. The person's perception of progress can be compared with the leader's observations of possible gains. There are many behaviors that cannot be readily observed, such as relative changes in thought or imagery patterns. Again, gains in these areas can be evaluated by simple questions. If questionnaires are to be the primary mode of evaluation, it has been recommended that they be administered frequently (Barlow et al., 1984). Many forms of brief questionnaires can be completed after each session.

In many types of common-theme groups the participants have been asked to complete tasks, or maintain a log between sessions. Logs provide good information for the leaders to monitor progress. The concreteness of the record-keeping requirements is helpful for providing additional motivation for the individual.

Another useful evaluative process is to use part of the closing time to have each member briefly and verbally assess progress. The estimate of change can be followed with each person stating how the group can help them make more progress. Used as a closing exercise, the verbal evaluation provides a problem-solving focus, and invites everyone to become more involved in assisting each other's progress.

FEEDBACK ON THE GROUP PROCESS

A few items in the assessment can be used to determine how the individual members perceive the group dynamics. The answers to these questions can give the leader a good feel for the group climate, whether anyone is at risk, and what is working most effectively. A variety of simple and quick devices has been employed as part of a feedback procedure.

A *Most Important Events* questionnaire (Bloch, Reibstein, & Crouch, 1979) provides a good alternative for routine evaluation. This device asks the person to recall the one event in the past three meetings that was most consequential for them, and to talk about the circumstances involved. The answers can then be classified according to the curative factors or other variables. One variation which could be used at the end of meetings has been suggested by

MacKenzie (1983). He asked group members to recall the incident that was most important to them during the most recent session.

Another brief evaluation technique involves defining the therapeutic factors at a language level appropriate to the group and have the members rate their relative importance after each meeting. The form asks each member to rate the factors on a five-point scale from Strongly Agree to Strongly Disagree. This particular version of the scale provides data about how central a particular curative factor was for a person during the group. The scale may be administered, with slight wording changes, at the end of a program or to evaluate a specific group session (Andrews, 1991).

In The Group Today:

_____ I learned something important about myself. (self-understanding)

_____ I felt valued and supported by the group leaders. (acceptance)

_____ I revealed highly personal information. (self-disclosure)

_____ I received valuable information, advice or suggestions. (guidance)

_____ I felt valued and supported by the other group members. (acceptance)

_____ I felt other group members had similar problems and feelings. (universality)

_____ I found it satisfying to help others. (altruism)

_____ I learned something important about myself by observing someone else. (vicarious learning)

_____ I shared personal feelings which brought me a sense of relief. (catharsis)

_____ I felt more hopeful about the future. (hope)

_____ I learned a new way of interacting with others. (LIA)

Please circle the *one* statement in the preceding list which describes the experience of most value for you today.

It is helpful to obtain both leaders' and members' ratings on the acceptance factor. As was previously discussed, acceptance is a critical factor and it is essential that the evaluation assess how the members are reacting to each other and the leaders. The last question, which asks the participant to circle one of the statements, is an attempt to get the person to indicate which factor was associated with the most learning.

Not all of the items need to be asked every week, but the questionnaire is so brief that little is gained by omitting items. The form can easily be modified to assess every two or three sessions, or be used as a postgroup or follow-up evaluation.

At times, it is helpful to add an item which requests feedback for the leader or leaders, for example:

List three words or phrases that describe _____'s leadership.

Feedback is most effective if gathered on each leader, and it is interesting to see how the group perceives each leader's style. Other similar devices are also effective. An adjective checklist can be constructed, and members asked to indicate which words apply to the leader (or leaders), for example warm, cold, helpful, critical, supportive, and so forth.

It is very useful to look at individual response patterns when evaluating the groups. The following evaluations were conducted at the end of short-term groups and the differences in the ratings by participants provided examples of how the scales may be used for analysis. The scoring is tabulated so individual patterns may be viewed. As presented, these data represent clinical data, and there is not sufficient empirical support to warrant any firm conclusions about the patterns of scores. The purpose is to illustrate how simple, locally devised instruments can be of value in analyzing and designing groups. If used routinely at the end of group sessions, it can (1) warn the leader about people in trouble, and (2) suggest a shift in emphasis in therapeutic factors to more effectively develop the dynamics of the group.

Group I

Group I focused on self-esteem issues for women, and was led by two women who were noted for their warm and supportive style.

Major Objectives for the Group

1. Create an accepting and supportive atmosphere in the group.

2. Develop each participant's awareness of patterns of negative thoughts, images, feelings, and behavior.

3. Assist each member to learn more positive patterns of thinking, feeling, imaging, or behaving.

4. Develop more adaptive stressor response patterns for each person.

Leaders' Analyses

Both leaders felt good about the group's first two sessions. They described it as cohesive and supportive with little conflict. The level of participation was high, and no unusual incidents were described. The leaders felt they worked well together. In their view, the first objective, that of support and acceptance, had been largely accomplished, and a substantial portion of the other three aims had been met in the first two meetings. Anonymous feedback from the members indicated the following. The higher the score (1–5), the more the member felt that the particular factor was present in the group during the session.

Therapeutic Factors	*Members' Ratings*						
	A	B	C	D	E	F	G
Acceptance (leaders)	5	5	5	5	5	5	5
Acceptance (members)	5	4	4	5	5	5	4
Universality	5	4	3	3	4	4	3
Self-disclosure	5	2	5	4	3	5	2
LIA	4	2	2	2	3	2	2
Altruism	5	3	4	5	4	4	2
Catharsis	4	3	2	4	1	4	3
Insight	5	2	5	5	4	5	4
Hope	4	4	3	4	3	5	3
Vicarious learning	5	1	4	3	3	2	2
Guidance	5	2	5	3	2	3	3

Progress on Objectives

Awareness of current patterns	4	4	3	2	1	3	4
Awareness of new patterns	3	2	3	2	1	3	2
New interpersonal responses	1	1	3	1	2	2	3
Support and acceptance	See Acceptance/						
	Universality scores						

Participants' Feedback on Leaders

Three words or phrases that describe Jenny's leadership:

good	supportive (3)*	informed
very good	challenging	warm and caring
great	non-aggressive	gentle (3)
respectful	perceptive	relaxed
wise	gentle but firm	understanding

Three words or phrases that describe Clara's leadership:

relaxed	sense of fun	gentle (2)	aware
helpful	caring (2)	understanding	good
humorous	encouraging	very good	
supportive (4)	perceptive	knowledgeable	great

In this case the leaders established a high level of acceptance in the brief group. Universality was not as high, but that probably was due to the nature of the problem focus rather than indicating any type of difficulty. The atmosphere in the group was certainly positive and supportive. The variance in the self-disclosure scores would be normal for this type of group and may have been due to time factors or personal styles of participants. Further investigation might determine why there was a difference. However, there was a reasonable amount of expression of feelings (catharsis).

The members seemed to be involved with each other for the most part (altruism), but there was little actually learned (LIA) about new ways of behaving from interactions in the group. The level of reported insight was quite high. However, the insight did not appear to relate well to the objectives for the group as evidenced by the *current patterns* and *new patterns* ratings. It may very well be that the insight had to do with issues associated with acceptance and universality instead. The level of vicarious learning was low as was the reception of new information (guidance).

As reported by the leaders, the group was quite cohesive. There was the suggestion that probably one or two members (B and G) were not very actively involved (low scores on altruism, self-disclosure, catharsis, and LIA). This was in contrast with A, who reported high scores on all factors. The differences would not

*Numbers in parentheses indicate the frequency with which word was used.

be a major concern because of the high level of leader and member acceptance for both members. Participant B and G may not have learned a lot, but there was little danger of either being a casualty. The picture presented by this group seems to be one of a warm accepting atmosphere, a reasonable amount of self-disclosure, and members responding to the disclosures with both support and positive feedback. These conditions lead to a high level of learning obtained through insight although the nature of the insight is unknown.

Future Design

The design implications from the feedback are reasonably clear. A good foundation of acceptance has been generated, but it would be helpful to consider ways of increasing the level of learning from interpersonal actions. LIA is one of the main vehicles for gain in a group of this type. In this case more LIA will help accomplish the fourth objective, which was learning new ways of interpersonal responding. The leaders' analysis overestimated the level of learning, probably because of the style and interpersonal needs of the coleaders. As a result, members may learn a lot about being supportive, but they may not learn much about conflict. Handling conflict situations without being self-critical is a key part of enhancing self-esteem and was a listed objective for the group.

The leaders were not planning to foster conflict, but the inevitable disagreements which sooner or later become a part of any group's development can be used for creating opportunities for LIA. Alternatively, the leaders might try to design role-playing situations where interpersonal conflict is a theme. In general the leaders would want to look for more opportunities to give *interpersonal* feedback to the group about *how* they are interacting. The leaders also need to encourage less active members to get involved. To this point members A, D, and F reported elevated levels of activity (high scores on altruism, self-disclosure, and catharsis) compared to the others, and perhaps some pairing of group members for work might help to spread the level of involvement.

One additional strategy for evaluation might have been considered after the next session. This group illustrated a situation where an open-ended questionnaire asking the participants *how* they learned would have been helpful in planning future processes in the group.

Group II

This group was led by a man and woman. In contrast to Group I, these leaders were known to be cognitive in their approach, and much more confrontive in their style. Both leaders had a background in which their groups emphasized educational purposes rather than therapeutic processes. The group was directed toward increasing personal awareness of issues related to chemical dependency.

Major Objectives

Increase the participants' awareness of:

1. the etiology of addiction.
2. how personal styles impact on work with clients with problems with chemical dependency.
3. what personal attitudes might interfere in work with chemically dependent clients.
4. major concerns evidenced by chemically dependent clients.

Leaders' Analyses

Immediately following the first session, the two leaders expressed a lot of frustration about the group members and the process. They found the participants to be non-responsive, and in their view not interested in the topic, despite all of them being volunteers for the group. Both leaders talked about having to "pull teeth" to get any interaction going and expressed their disappointment about what had happened. After some discussion, they came to the conclusion that they had been overly controlling and too confrontive. They decided to greatly reduce their input in the second session and try to be more supportive and affirming in the interaction. The following feedback was obtained after the second session.

Therapeutic Factors	*Members' Ratings*					
	A	B	C	D	E	F
Acceptance (leaders)	3	5	3	4	4	5
Acceptance (members)	5	3	4	4	5	2
Universality	4	4	3	3	3	2
Self-disclosure	3	2	2	3	3	3

LIA	1	5	3	3	1	4
Altruism	3	2	4	4	2	3
Catharsis	1	3	3	3	2	2
Insight	5	4	3	2	5	1
Hope	3	2	2	4	3	3
Vicarious learning	4	4	3	2	2	1
Guidance	5	5	4	5	5	5

Progress on Objectives

Understanding of etiology	4	4	5	4	5	5
Awareness of personal style	2	3	1	1	2	3
Attitudes and feelings	3	2	2	2	2	1
Major concerns	5	4	4	4	5	5

Three words or phrases that describe Brad's leadership:

confronting (2)*
professional and clear (2)
elaborated too much on framework
motivated, enjoyed what he was doing
tendency to get bogged down on detail
confusing in first session
lots of information (2)

Three words or phrases that describe Kathy's leadership:

clear and knowledgeable   no problems
invested interest in the subject
informative (2)   open
confident (3)   self-disclosing
supportive (2)   professional (2)

   The contrasting scores on acceptance and guidance are indicative of the whole group. There was apparently an emphasis on providing usable information, and the participants rated that aspect highly. Furthermore, the input did lead to some insights for two or three members. Most of the other scales suggested that little group cohesion developed (low universality, LIA, self-disclosure and altruism), and the actual curative powers of a group were not

---

*Numbers in parentheses indicate the frequency with which word was used.

effectively utilized. The level of acceptance scores were a concern, and the possibility of some negative outcomes must be considered, particularly for member F. The two leaders' need to have control of the process got out of hand. If the ratings had been obtained after the first meeting they probably would have looked even worse. At a minimum, it is clear that the leaders' need to provide information prevented much development, or use of, the curative powers of the group. In general, the descriptions of the leaders confirmed the members' ratings on the therapeutic factors. Most of the feedback about leadership focused on their input rather than interaction.

Summary of Analysis

The differences between the members' perceptions of the leaders of Group I and Group II were striking. Group I descriptions (warm, caring, gentle) emphasized the affective strengths of the leaders. For Group II, cognitive factors (clear, informative, and knowledgable) were dominant. The two groups represented contrary leadership styles. The leader characteristics produced one group where their emphasis was too much on personal comfort, whereas the other focused excessively on providing information.

Both groups could have been considered successful to some extent, particularly Group I. In both cases, the feedback allowed modifications in the styles and process in the groups. The Group II leaders, despite their initial difficulties, were able to see that they had not been "stuck with a bunch of losers," but their operating style had a lot to do with the negative experience in session one.

The two critiques are examples of informal types of evaluations which may be conducted while a group is in progress. The questionnaire required little time to administer, and the information provided assistance to the leaders. Most importantly, the leaders were able to compare their perceptions of the process with the members, and eliminate much of the guesswork involved in developing the future group design.

Summary of Continuing Evaluation

- Leaders
  - review major thoughts and feelings

- — discuss any coleader problems
- — provide feedback to each other

- General Process
  - — relate issues to group development
  - — identify major group issues and incidents
  - — use behavior-consequences-meaning model for problems

- Review major personal issues for each member
  - — check individual acceptance

- Review major interpersonal issues in the group
- Review feedback from participants on objectives and dynamics

7

ETHICAL BEHAVIOR AND GROUP LEADERSHIP

Complexities inherent in group work create issues that make ethical practice more difficult. Most professional ethical guidelines emphasize the welfare of the consumer in a dyadic intervention. Such principles rarely consider specific group situations that may create different or unusual types of ethical problems.

Although the protection of the consumer is still a primary concern for all helping specialties, difficulties are compounded by the lack of comprehensive guidelines for group work for many professionals. In addition to psychologists, it is not unusual for psychiatrists, social workers, counselors of all types, nurses, and occupational therapists to be involved in leading groups. The variety of professionals involved in group leadership means that standards of training are different, and each profession is governed by its own unique code of ethics. Psychologists who colead groups with other professionals may find conflict between different sets of ethical requirements. When coleaders represent different professions, they must plan carefully to avoid possible breaches of ethical requirements.

Additionally, many psychologists will become involved with groups led by paraprofessional or lay people. The proliferation of self-help groups (see Chapter 1) is an example of increasing cooperation between psychologists and lay group leaders. In many circumstances, nonprofessional leaders will have no ethical principles other than tradition to guide their practice. Psychologists who consult, train, or lead groups offered by self-help organizations will find ethical practice is more difficult. A psychologist involved with such groups will have to exercise considerable vigilance to protect clients.

Ethical Codes and Group Practice

No portion of the APA *Ethical Principles of Psychologists and Code of Conduct* (1992) applies solely to group work. Of course, the general requirements of the APA *Ethical Principles* apply in all therapeutic situations. Actions consistent with ethical behavior apply in widely different circumstances, such as in group therapy. In addition, the APA previously published *Guidelines for Psychologists Conducting Growth Groups* (1973) which were meant to be applied to particular types of groups described by the generic name of "Growth Groups." The latter publication was developed in response to the dramatic expansion of group practice in the 1960s. In current practice, the APA *Ethical Principles* (1992) are the primary resource for psychologists who plan and lead common-theme or general therapy groups.

An additional ethical resource has proven to be useful. There are some psychologists active in group work who endorse, and promote, the ethical framework developed by the Association for Specialists in Group Work (ASGW) (see for example, Corey & Corey, 1987; Lakin, 1985). The ASGW *Ethical Guidelines for Group Counselors* (1989) offers specific standards for group practice. The ASGW *Ethical Guidelines* is divided into 16 major categories, which are detailed and prescriptive. The ASGW statements extend and clarify the leader's thinking about ethical dilemmas, and if followed, can prevent many problems from occurring.

Protection of the client in dyadic or group therapy often involves similar decisions and processes. A thoughtful and consistent adherence to general ethical principles assures proper behavior in almost any circumstance. Nevertheless, there are ethical issues unique to group operations and they are considered in the following discussion. Ethical concerns that arise during pregroup planning, the ongoing group process, and termination and follow-up will be highlighted. For each ethical problem, applicable sections of the APA *Ethical Principles* (1992) and the ASGW *Ethical*

Guidelines (1989) are considered. Relevant ethical cases discussed by the APA Ethics Committee and published in the *Casebook on Ethical Principles of Psychologists* (1987) are cited.

ETHICAL CONCERNS IN PLANNING GROUPS

Competence of Leaders

Principle A of the APA Code, with Standard 1.04 requires the practitioner to be aware of professional limitations and to provide services only when they are qualified to do so. Competence is a concern in any type of psychological work, but there is a special case for emphasizing it in group work due to the potential for harm. As Keith-Spiegel and Koocher (1985) noted.

> *The group therapist has considerably less control over the content and direction of the therapeutic session than does the individual therapist. As a result, there is greater potential for individuals in the group to have unfavorable or adverse experiences . . . Problems might include stresses resulting from confrontation, criticism, threats to confidentiality, or even development of a dependency on the group (p. 135–136).*
>
> *In many ways, the group therapist's ethical burden is far greater than the individual therapist's, since the psychologist conducting group therapy must consider the psychological ecology of the therapy or program as it affects different participants (p.137).*

There are possibilities of damage to a person in a group which do not arise in a dyadic setting. A special type of knowledge or expertise is required for *group therapy*, as opposed to education in groups. Groups are potent forces for both positive and negative change. An inexperienced leader needs to consider carefully which additional safeguards are necessary to protect members during the experience.

Unfortunately, there is the tendency for some employers to assume there is an automatic transfer of expertise from individual to group therapy. Psychologists are employed in settings where they are asked to design and lead groups regardless of their prior training or experience.

Organizational and Individual Conflicts

Standard 8.03 of the APA *Ethical Principles* requires that a psychologist be aware when there are possible conflicts between organizational constraints or demands and the Code. If such a conflict arises, the practitioner must affirm her or his commitment to ethical practice *and* attempt to resolve the identified conflict. The psychologist must not allow such pressures to lead to a misuse of his or her influence (Standard 1.15).

An example of organizational pressures affecting the welfare of the client is when a program manager decides it is more cost effective to treat people in groups. The APA *Casebook* reported a situation (Case 1.d.2) where the Ethics Committee censured a psychologist for arbitrarily increasing the number of groups which made less time available for individual work. The fact that the change was ordered by a nonpsychologist was not considered an adequate defense.

Group treatment may be suitable for some individuals, but the routine placement of people into group treatment modalities for economic reasons alone is obviously unacceptable practice and does little to protect the welfare of the client (Principle E). Regardless of work pressures, the psychologist must select clients that can profit from a group experience.

Other examples of organizational pressures influencing programs include people in prison settings, individuals convicted of drug offenses, and children with behavior problems in schools. Often such people are referred to groups on a nonvoluntary basis. Whether or not such referrals are accepted for treatment needs careful consideration. It is not unusual to develop programs because a local community (or subculture) has decided that such people need treatment. In some cases societal pressure may lead to legislation or regulations that create conflicts for the practitioner. Nonvoluntary requirements for treatment, such as with sexual offenders, is not uncommon.

A nonvoluntary client may find it relatively easy to avoid meaningful participation in dyadic therapy. Avoiding purposeful interaction in a group setting is more difficult because of the possibility of substantial peer pressure to participate. Some leaders may be tempted to allow or use the group to coerce the reluctant client in an attempt to achieve a more favorable outcome. Such temptations need to be resisted for both ethical and practical reasons. Coercion violates ethical standards and rarely produces meaningful change. Leaders of groups which contain nonvoluntary participants must consider carefully their options and probable outcomes. When does the creation of an "invitation to participate" become coercion? Are nonvolunteers encouraged to express their feelings about their lack of freedom? What happens to the person who refuses to become involved in the group process?

Lakin (1985) suggested that when coerced clients are part of a group, the leader should make the nonvoluntary nature of the referral part of the group. With this approach, the fact that members are required to participate becomes the first group agenda item. The alternative, to sustain the pretence that a particular person is present because they want to be there, is detrimental to the group. Forced attendance will become a covert agenda if it is not dealt with openly in the group. In any case, it is unlikely that the psychologist is exempted from the requirement of informed consent (Standard 4.02) in the event of a nonvoluntary participant.

Clients may not have a choice whether to attend or not, but they have a right to know what will happen, the probable consequences of the treatment and what will happen with new information the psychologist obtains during the treatment. There is a clear requirement that the leaders clarify issues such as roles and limits of confidentiality when providing services at the request of a third party (Standard 1.21). The ASGW *Ethical Guidelines* are more explicit, and require that the leaders clarify all the parameters of nonvoluntary participation, including informed consent procedures and reporting requirements.

There are also occasions when legal requirements may conflict with ethical requirements of confidentiality. For instance, some individuals receive court orders mandating treatment and judicial systems often require reports on progress. Principle 5.05 allows disclosure without consent when " . . . mandated by law." In such cases the psychologist must inform the client of the specific type of report required and its potential impact prior to treatment.

Outpatient treatment of sex offenders is another example of a situation where certain types of self-disclosure require a report to outside authorities to protect the welfare of minors. Often the therapist must inform the client about reporting requirements and procedures before treatment, and effective treatment cannot proceed without informed consent.

Advertising Groups

In the past psychologists have not actively solicited clients for therapy. Most practitioners do not consider direct soliciting to be ethical, and the APA Code prohibits uninvited in-person solicitation of psychotherapy patients ". . . who because of their particular circumstances are vulnerable to undue influence (Standard 3.06)." However, the 1992 Federal Trade Commission order has effectively removed many of the previous restrictions on advertising. It is possible to actively recruit clients as long as the advertisements are truthful.

If a group is advertised, there is an obligation that the psychologist must specify ". . . appropriate information beforehand about the nature of such services . . ." (Standard 1.07). *Informed choice* is the best guideline to use in announcing group programs. The applicant needs to know why the group is conducted, the therapist's goals, and the qualifications of its leaders.

A related issue is the type of group that is advertised. Keith-Spiegel and Koocher (1985) expressed concern about advertisements which fail to distinguish between education and therapy. Obviously, different ethical requirements apply if a professional is advertising therapy. They recommend that people who conduct publicly advertised sessions be very clear about their goals. If the advertised program involves education, but no therapy, the ads should reflect that. If the leader intends to offer psychotherapy, individual clients should not be solicited.

The APA *Casebook* reported an extreme example of a psychologist who advertised a personal growth group but did not indicate that the experience would require communal swimming and massage while nude (Case 4.d.). The leader was censured and warned not to conduct further groups unless her advertisements clearly ". . . describe her philosophy of treatment and explain the rationale for the activities . . ." (p.57).

Informed Consent

As the preceding case demonstrated, the potential group member should be fully aware of the nature of the group and its anticipated processes (Standards 1.07 and 4.02). Although in the past many groups have recruited members solely based upon a brochure, the need for informed consent seems to require a face-to-face contact. In addition, properly evaluating the person's suitability for a group (Principle E: Concern for Other's Welfare) suggests the need for an interview process. It is extremely doubtful whether a written advertisement could adequately accomplish either requirement, much less both.

In addition to proper advertising, the best way to insure that the potential participant has made an informed choice is to conduct a proper intake interview to assess the person's readiness for group work and gain informed consent. A structured intake interview seems to be a minimum condition.

Confidentiality

Ethical requirements for confidentiality require actions unique to group work. The leader can behave in a perfectly ethical manner yet cannot guarantee the behavior of the other participants. All the leader can do is ask the participants to respect confidentiality, and reiterate its importance occasionally. This problem should be emphasized as part of the intake procedure and repeated during the first session. The limits of group confidentially must be explained before the group begins except in unusual circumstances (Standard 5.01). Even though all members may contract initially to respect confidentiality, the prospective member needs to know the original agreement does not provide a guarantee of protection.

The ASGW *Ethical Guidelines* are more extensive and require the leader to explain clearly the limits and parameters associated with confidentiality. The therapist must instruct participants about the difficulties involved in group confidentiality, including the consequences if an intentional breach should occur. The latter requirement means the leader has to anticipate a violation of confidentiality, and predetermine how to handle it if it occurs. If a violation becomes known to the participants, the episode becomes part of the process and the entire group must address the violation.

Additional ASGW Pregroup Requirements

ASGW *Ethical Guidelines* (ASGW, 1989) require leaders to perform several functions prior to the group. Leaders must provide complete information about their credentials, group objectives, possible dual treatment situations, fee contracting, and potential limitations of the group experience. In addition, leaders must:

1.   Explore the risks of personal changes and the prospective member's ability to face them.
2.   Indicate who is the primary author of the group goals. That is, do the objectives reflect (for example) institutional goals, legal requirements, or parental expectations? The participant's possible role in modifying the stated goals must be clarified.
3.   Guarantee that they ". . . consider the financial status and locality of prospective group members" (p. 120). Leaders must consider whether participants can afford customary fees and if they live in reasonable proximity to the group setting. The latter requirements are apparently an attempt to insure that public agencies are reasonably responsive to community needs.
4.   Use individual, group, or team interviews, or a written questionnaire to conduct an orientation to the group.
5.   Establish and communicate procedures used for terminating group treatment. Members may leave the group when they wish and are encouraged to discuss their leaving with the leader and the group. However, it is the leader's responsibility to make sure the group does not ". . . use undue pressure to force a member to remain in the group" (ASGW, *Ethical Guidelines*, p. 122).

It is obvious that the ASGW requirements place considerable responsibility for appropriate planning on the leaders of a group. The specificity and scope of the guidelines require extensive thought while planning the group design and process. Although such pregroup requirements are not explicitly required for APA members, the ASGW *Ethical Guidelines* are very useful for planning. If followed, there is no question that the leader has made every effort to conduct a planned group ethically and responsibly.

Training Students

A special type of planning is required when groups occur within academic settings and the experience is an integral part of the student's training. Participation in a group naturally requires some types of self-disclosures by members. Therefore, there is a possibility that a student's admission of personal problems may be viewed negatively by those who administer the program. Students who honestly admit their psychological liabilities may put themselves at risk.

In one circumstance a professor taught a group course which required the students to attend a therapy group which the professor led. A graduate student filed ethical charges protesting the arrangement, which were upheld by the APA Ethics Committee. The professor was censured and required to publish a syllabus that correctly described the course. The Ethics Committee instructed him to avoid dual relationships in the future. The Committee found that if a group experience was required, the leader could not be associated with the training program in which the group was offered. A similar situation involved a clinical faculty member who required group therapy as part of the training of graduate students. In the Committee's view such an arrangement created a dual relationship. They censured the psychologist in question (Case 6.a.4). Requiring a student to attend a group experience led by a faculty member responsible for the student's assessment in any part of the program was found to be unethical. Even if the student's participation in the group was not assessed in any way, the Committee felt that the potential for an unhelpful multiple relationship was present (Standard 1.17). The faculty member who leads a student group also risks problems because of the power differences between the two parties (Principle E). If a group experience is essential for training students, the wisest course is to use a leader who has no association with the training program. Opportunities for violations of confidentiality, abuse of power and harmful dual relationships (Principle B) are minimized by such an arrangement.

The ASGW *Ethical Guidelines* deviates from the APA *Ethical Principles* on the issue of training group leaders. ASGW allows students to participate in a group, which is consistent with the APA view. However, it appears that the instructors of such courses may lead such groups by ". . . separating course grades from participation in the group and by allowing students to decide what issues to explore and when to stop" (ASGW, *Ethical Guidelines*, p. 124).

It is difficult to determine the best option when considering whether academic staff can lead groups which contain their students. In the technical sense, this practice constitutes a dual relationship. Even the requirement that participation not be graded does not remove the possibility that a faculty member could demonstrate bias toward a student in another course or setting. More positively, staff-led groups of students can provide substantial opportunities for learning. Instructors can be much more aware of the areas where the students need training, and have more opportunities to remediate shortcomings. Additionally, many training programs conducted outside colleges and universities require trainers both to teach and evaluate trainees.

Overall, the APA position on academic training seems most convincing. The complete separation of academic evaluation and clinical material gained in groups is essential. Despite the best intentions of the faculty members, there is no way they can *guarantee* they will view students objectively if they reveal personal material in a group, or if students come into conflict with them. As in all groups, the welfare of the participants must come first, and all efforts must be made to protect them. There is no convincing reason that requires students give up this right.

ETHICAL ISSUES DURING THE GROUP

In addition to the ethical issues which arise during planning, groups have some unique characteristics which naturally foster potentially difficult ethical conflicts. Group leaders are required to exercise considerable vigilance to protect the clients' welfare as much as possible. Lakin (1986; 1991) has outlined several key differences between group and dyadic approaches which influence the nature of ethical practice. Some of the most important distinctions include the following:

1.   The group climate is a powerful force and certain behaviors are supported or punished by the members in a way that is qualitatively different from how the individual therapist might respond. The group will develop a consensus about reality which may tend to exclude some members.

In a normal culture there are diverse views about objective reality. As people enter groups they bring their own individual "truths" from their personal culture with them. These personalized beliefs create problems for the interpersonal process, particularly early in the group. It is much more difficult for the therapist to control these interactions and the possibility of members verbally abusing each other is a consideration (Kotter, 1982). As the group progresses, there is often the reconciling of differences and movement toward cohesion, which most leaders view as a desirable state. However, a cohesive group also constructs a powerful view of reality and does not easily tolerate contrary views. A member who develops an alternative view of group reality is at some risk, and the leader will have to be careful not to collude in suppressing an individual's discrepant perceptions. A cohesive group is a seductive group. It is all too easy to go along with the current consensus of reality rather than face the necessary conflict produced by a deviant member, or contrary views.

2. It is easy for the leader to become strongly influenced by the "group mood" which does not exist in individual work.

Groups sometimes get so infused with a particular feeling that it requires firm action to get them to examine the process they have created. Members may ignore obvious problems or force individuals to conform rather than violate the current atmosphere. Groups may use playful actions, humor, or strong supportive moods to avoid work or to circumvent problematic issues.

3. There are multiple opportunities for the exchanging of roles in groups. For example, suddenly a spectator may become the prime focus of the group, or a client may switch to a helping role. Such role exchanges are impossible in most dyadic work.

In any of these situations circumstances can develop that may be harmful to the client. Members may act as leaders, clients, support persons and antagonists all within one group meeting. Sudden switches from a spectator role to being the central focus can be particularly difficult to manage. The multiple roles are often confusing to people inexperienced in group work. In addition, the well documented difficulty that even experienced leaders have in accurately determining how individuals are responding to the group must be considered (see for example (Budman et al., 1987; Dies & Teleska 1985; Hausman, 1979; Lieberman et al., 1973). Leaders need to be aware of the difficulty individuals may have switching from one role to another, and be able to assist them when necessary.

Personal and Therapeutic Bias

Standards 1.08 and 2.04(c) require an awareness of human differences and a sensitivity to how ignorance or bias might negatively affect the provision of services. Personal bias becomes even more pronounced in a group setting because of the power differential. Older men or women are dismissed beneath a stereotype. Minorities are subjected to the needs of the majority in the same way they are outside the group. Individuals from different socioeconomic groups, in particular the lower ones, are patronized or ignored because their speech, mannerisms, or dress are different from the rest of the group. Cultural or ethnic differences are ignored and the idea of "one treatment for all" is perpetuated. Often the problem is not that the leaders have demonstrated bias, but that they have allowed subtle evidence of it by group members to go unchallenged. The dynamics of all forms of prejudice are very much part of a group, since it represents a microcosm of society.

The multicultural nature of the United States and other Western countries mean that leaders increasingly will face group membership other than from the white-middle or upper classes. Culturally mixed groups will become more prevalent and require different strategies. Unfortunately, there are few guidelines available for leaders working with culturally diverse people. The few reports that do exist provide evidence of how difficult it can be for the uninformed psychologist to provide culturally responsive services.

Delgado (1983) has outlined several cultural dynamics which affect Hispanics particularly in group psychotherapeutic situations. For example, Hispanics are unlikely to trust organizations in the community but will respond to personal relationships. This finding implies that recruitment for groups involves a more personal outreach type of methodology, rather than depending on Hispanics to respond to an organization's invitation to participate. Hispanics prefer groups that are action oriented and include natural support systems as part of the solution to current difficulties. Treating Hispanic sex offenders adds further difficulties, particularly when they are primarily Spanish-speaking. Hispanic men are very reluctant to discuss their sexuality in a group setting and are often unwilling to openly criticize each other (Cullen & Travin, 1990).

Other authors (Tsui & Shultz, 1988) have warned that Asian clients perceive group situations quite differently from Caucasians. Often they perceive common group behavior, such as self-disclosure or providing feedback to others, as violations of traditional values. Asian group members also are sensitive to power relationships, such as how others view them as a minority.

A group designed for Southeast Asian refugees, with primary diagnoses of schizophrenia or depression, conclusively illustrated the difficulties Caucasian psychologists have with a significantly different culture. In order for the group to function properly, therapists soon had to separate the patients by ethnic group and in some cases by gender, as well. During the process, Asian views of authority often resulted in members deferring to the authority of the group leaders, and being reluctant to initiate interaction in the group. Asian members expected leaders to provide solutions, in contrast to the Western view that the group develops until it can solve its own problems. In some circumstances women were reluctant to contribute unless the men gave them permission to speak. Similarly, younger members were very hesitant to talk unless their elders had already expressed their views.

Of particular note was one incident where a relaxation procedure involved dim lights and hushed voices. During the procedure the members became very anxious and the leaders had to stop the activity. The leaders discovered that their relaxation process was similar to shamanistic rituals often used in the refugees' country (Kinzie et al., 1988).

When the entire group membership represents a different culture, disability, or sexual preference, there is an opportunity for the leaders to learn about the differences and still conduct the process effectively. Often the dissimilar person may be a minority in the group and the prejudice more subtle. Without proper awareness by the leader it is easy for such participants to become isolated, ignored, or patronized. Although leaders cannot be an expert on every subculture, they can seek training or consultation when necessary and develop appropriate referral resources. It is the leader's responsibility to understand the ethnic and cultural issues which may impact on the person's behavior in a group setting. Without knowledge of the client's essential values, the leader's intervention can suggest an action which increases the level of conflict between the person and his or her culture. Consequently, what the majority culture may view as increased mental health will actually exacerbate the person's distress.

Corey, Corey, and Callanan (1990) cited an example of how a leader may respond to a person who is unhappy in a marriage, but the individual's reference culture demands that the family remain intact. Most Caucasian psychologists would support the idea that people need to work through guilt or dependency issues in order to decide whether to leave a marriage. Nevertheless, such a suggestion promotes the idea that the person should consider divorce. The assumption is that guilt or dependency needs are barriers to the possibility of separation, which the person must resolve. However, the important consideration may be the clash between the cultural requirements and personal needs, not the decision to leave or stay in the marriage. If the leader is not aware of the normal pressures in the person's culture, the intervention can increase the degree of conflict rather than ameliorate it.

Personal State of the Leader

Groups are more risky for leaders with personal problems because of the extent of damage the dysfunctional leader can inflict. For example, a person allowed to become a scapegoat during the group process is not only rejected by the professional leader, but by a group of supposed peers. The negative impact of such an experience can be devastating, and the power differential in a group setting can intensify the emotional impact.

The leader's inappropriate needs for control, approval, or seduction (to name just a few issues), create problems for everyone, not just the people who might be the target. Inviting dependency relationships because of the therapist's need for control is a common trap. High needs for approval can result in different kinds of problems. It is only natural that ". . . therapists are more prone to give more time, attention, and to be more responsive to group members whom they find personally reinforcing" (Gregory & McConnell, 1986, p. 60). Finally, the seductive group leader not only creates difficulties for the group member, but can disrupt the entire group process.

Unfortunately, there is no easy solution to the therapist's personal problems intruding in the group. As is usual in any therapeutic endeavor, the best prevention involves good training prior to the group and continual consultation or supervision during it. As Standard 1.13 requires, group leaders need to be aware they are not immune to personal problems and that their particular conflicts can harm others. When the leader becomes aware of dysfunctional behavior, the options are termination of professional activities, therapy, or consultation with a colleague. Coleadership is an excellent way of avoiding such problems. Having another competent professional actually present in the group is the preferred option. With dual leaders, inappropriate interpersonal difficulties can be observed and suitable remedial actions initiated.

Dual Therapeutic Regimens

One other circumstance which easily can involve an ethical problem is where a client is already involved in therapy and applies to enter a group with a psychologist. It becomes the second therapist's responsibility to handle the situation by discussions with the client that "minimize the risk of confusion and conflict and through consultation with the other service providers as needed" (Standard 4.04).

The APA *Casebook* described an instance where a psychologist conducted individual therapy with a client who was in group therapy conducted by a psychiatrist. The psychologist knew about the dual therapeutic relationships but took no action. Although the client apparently was not harmed, the Ethics Committee forcefully reminded the psychologist of the requirement to work cooperatively with other professionals in such circumstances.

Individual and group therapy offered to supplement each other can be a very effective and powerful treatment strategy. It is also easy to imagine that clients can be confused by two different therapeutic regimens which are uncoordinated. Managing a client in two different treatment modalities can be quite difficult, as well as time-consuming. However, there is little choice in the matter. In addition to cooperative treatment relationships the welfare of the consumer (Principle E) also applies.

ASGW Requirements During the Group

The ASGW *Ethical Guidelines* are definite on what is expected of the leader conducting a group. One of the major tenets is the distinction between therapeutic forces and undue pressure from the leader or members. Although there may be difficulty in separating the two group forces, the leader needs to be alert to the possibility of undue pressure. Leaders can encourage the development of therapeutic forces, such as feelings of acceptance, universality, or altruism. Group pressure is qualitatively different from encouragement. Leaders or members who prescribe behavior, punish deviations from their norms, or strongly and exclusively reinforce actions which perpetuate their standards, are exerting pressure.

In addition to being aware of group pressures, the leader must take care to avoid imposing personal values on the group. Personal values are separate from group values. The ASGW feels there are values common to a well functioning group that the leader should communicate to the prospective member. They ". . . include expressing feelings, being direct and honest, sharing personal material with others, learning how to trust, improving interpersonal communication, and deciding for oneself" (ASGW *Ethical Guidelines*, p. 123). However, the leader's personal beliefs about marriage, religion, and politics are not common to groups, and need to be separate from the process.

ASGW requirements depart from most other codes in its attempt to indicate which values are inherently part of a group process. The requirement that therapists educate potential members about specific values is an interesting development and has some obvious theoretical implications.

Leaders must avoid using the group for their personal therapy, and the leader is prohibited from employing the group experience as a substitute for personal development. Implicit in this requirement is the concern that troubled leaders may use the group to work out their personal issues, instead of focusing on the problems of the members. There is nothing wrong with a leader personally benefiting from a group's experience. Nevertheless, any personal gain by a leader should arise from serendipity rather than by design. In other words, it seems questionable for leaders to make their own concerns or personal dynamics a focus of the group. The sole exception is probably when a leader's interpersonal behavior has a negative impact on the group. In such cases, the group leader can invite the participants to give feedback about their reactions to the leader, or utilize some other similar technique.

Other ASGW requirements include the need to: (a) safeguard the equitable use of group time; (b) prevent verbal or physical abuse, or inappropriate confrontations; (c) consider the use of a coleader for large groups; (d) develop and explain policies for between-group sessions with individual members; and (e) demonstrate awareness of appropriate community resources for referral purposes. These standards are clear evidence that the ASGW code not only proposes guidelines which prevent ethical problems, but prescribes the type of practice which will prevent the development of an ethical violation.

One other ASGW direction of importance requires leaders to be able to articulate a ". . . theoretical orientation that guides their practice and they are able to provide a rationale for their interventions" (ASGW, p. 124). This requirement means that the leader has to demonstrate some understanding of group dynamics and not just attempt to transfer dyadic therapy to a group situation. Moreover, the need for sound theory to guide practice is both recognized and promoted by the statement. Leaders with an understandable theoretical rationale are less likely to be caprcious or arbitrary in practice.

ETHICS: TERMINATION AND FOLLOW-UP

Psychologists terminate a professional relationship when it becomes reasonably clear that the patient or client no longer needs the service, is not benefiting, or is being harmed by continuing service (Standard 4.09[b]).

This standard can present a dilemma for the group leader. Suppose a person has contracted for a specified number of group therapy sessions. After a few weeks it becomes apparent that the person has gained nothing from the group, and there are minimal prospects for improvement. Ethically, the leader must suggest termination of the group treatment. However, removing the person from the group can affect its functioning, and may affect negatively the value of the other members' treatment. It can be detrimental to the person and the group when premature termination occurs. In particular, when a member leaves with no explanation it can disrupt the group's development. Groups are prone to express anxiety about the termination and often will spend considerable time speculating about why the person left. In some groups the missing person can influence the group process for a significant period of time.

Regardless of the potential disruptive effects, the member has the right to leave at any time. It is also the leader's responsibility to communicate that right, and to support it. Problems can be avoided if the right to leave, and the suggested procedures for leaving, are part of the informed consent process during the intake interview. Even if there is no notice of termination, most premature terminations can be handled successfully. In the normal course of living people occasionally are "left without notice." When premature termination occurs in a group there is an opportunity to handle the feelings of those left behind. The remaining members often display a variety of reactions, such as feelings of rejection, guilt and anger. These feelings are common in groups and can be processed in a useful way in the group as long as the focus of discussion remains on the *reactions* of the people who are left. Speculations about *why* the person did not return usually are nonproductive.

ASGW Assessment and Follow-Up

In addition to a clear and proper termination procedure, The ASGW *Ethical Guidelines* also require that a group be assessed and followed up to determine longer-term effects. Leaders must make attempts to assess the results of their group process and conduct follow-up research. The contacts may be personal, by phone, or in writing. The follow-up should include an evaluation of effects on the participants, members' goal attainment, and feedback for purposes of future design.

As is true with other parts of the code, this section is most explicit about the need for both outcome and formative research. The leader not only needs to know what happened in the completed group, but what might be helpful in designing new groups. Other codes encourage research, but the ASGW Guidelines clearly require leaders to continually evaluate what they do and the effect it has.

SUMMARY OF MAJOR ETHICAL STANDARDS

Overall, there is considerable agreement between the APA and ASGW codes about the ethical leadership of groups. Nevertheless, the ASGW *Ethical Guidelines* (1989) extend the requirements outlined in the APA *Ethical Principles* (1992). The added clarity and understanding offered by the ASGW is not surprising since many of its members are psychologists, and the code is written specifically for group practice. The two sets of guidelines not only assist with promoting ethical conduct in group work, but describe many of the essential components associated with effective group practice. The following statements summarize the essential requirements for planning and conducting group therapy.

1. All organizational requirements, constraints, and legal strictures need to be identified and reconciled prior to the group, if at all possible.

2. Leaders must be properly trained to conduct the planned group. The nature of the group, its objectives, and major processes must be developed clearly so they can be communicated to applicants.

3. Members should be carefully evaluated as to their suitability to profit from a group experience. In addition to the nature of the group, potential members should be informed of the education, training, and experience of the group leader(s). The principle of *informed consent* should guide the entire process.

4. The limits of confidentiality need to be clarified before and during the group.

5. Group members must have free choice to continue or terminate treatment. In situations where there is premature termination, the leader should take steps to ensure the person has sufficient resources or a proper referral, if necessary.

6. Group participation may be required of students as part of their training. If required, the nature and purpose of the groups should be clearly described, as well as possible negative effects. The group participation normally is not graded. Faculty associated with the training program in any way should not lead groups composed of students.

7. During the group leaders need to demonstrate:

   a. a sensitivity to possible bias related to human differences.
   b. understanding of group forces and how to prevent participants from being damaged by the process.
   c. awareness that their personal problems may impinge on the group members or process, and maintain a consultative relationship to monitor such a possibility.
   d. a clear theoretical perspective on group process and interventions.

REFERENCES

Abramson, H.A. (1979). Psychosomatic group therapy with parents of children with intractable asthma: X. The Peter's family: II. *Journal of Asthma Research, 16*(4), 149–164.

American Psychological Association. (1987). *Casebook on ethical principles of psychologists.* Washington, DC.

American Psychological Association. (1973). Guidelines for Psychologists Conducting Growth Groups. *American Psychologist 28,* 933.

American Psychological Association. (1992). Ethical principles of psychologists. *American Psychologist, 45*(3), 390–395.

Anderson, J.D. (1985). Working with groups: Little known facts that challenge well-known myths. *Small Group Behavior, 16*(3), 267–283.

Anderson, L. F., & Robertson, S. E. (1985). Group facilitation: Functions and skills. *Small Group Behaviour, 16*(2), 139–156.

Andrews, H. (1991). *Evaluating Ongoing Therapeutic Groups: Rationale and Process.* Presentation at the 25th Annual Conference of the Australian Psychological Society, Adelaide, South Australia.

Arnowitz, E., Brunswick, L., & Kaplan, B.H. (1983). Group therapy with patients in the waiting room of an oncology clinic. *Social Work, 28*(5), 395–397.

Association for Specialists in Group Work. (1989). Ethical guidelines for group counsellors. *The Journal for Specialists in Group Work, 15*(2), 119–126.

Barlow, D.H., Hayes, S.C., & Nelson, R.O. (1984). *The Scientific Practitioner.* Sydney: Pergamon Press.

Berne, E. (1966). *Principles of Group Treatment.* New York: Oxford University Press.

Bloch, S. (1987). Humor in group therapy. In W.F Fry and & W.A. Salameh, (Eds.), *Handbook of Humour and Psychotherapy* (pp 171–194). Sarasota, FL Professional Resources Exchange, Inc.

Bloch, S., & Crouch, E. (1985). *Therapeutic Factors in Group Psychotherapy.* Oxford: Oxford University Press.

Bloch, S., Reibstein, J., & Crouch, E. (1979). A method for the study of therapeutic factors in group psychotherapy. *British Journal of Psychiatry, 134,* 257–263.

Block, L.R. (1985). On potentiality and limits of time: The single-session group and the cancer patient. *Social Work with Groups, 8*(2), 81–99.

Bonney, W.C., Randall, D.A., & Cleveland, J.D. (1986). An analysis of client-perceived curative factors in a therapy group of former incest victims. *Small Group Behavior, 17*(3), 303–321.

Brandes, N.S. (1977). Group therapy is not for every adolescent: Two case illustrations. *International Journal of Group Psychotherapy, 27*(4), 507–510.

Budman, S.H. (1981). Significant treatment factors in short-term psychotherapy. *Group, 5,* 25–31.

Budman, S.H., Demby, A., Feldstein, M., and Redondo, J. (1987) Preliminary findings on a new instrument to measure cohesion in group psychotherapy. *International Journal of Group Psychotherapy, 37*(1) 75–94.

Budman, S.H., & Gurman, A.S. (1988). *Theory and practice of brief therapy.* New York: Guilford Press.

Burlingame, G.M., & Fuhriman, A. (1990). Time-limited group therapy. *Counselling Psychologist, 18*(1), 93–118.

Butler, T., & Fuhriman, A. (1983). Level of functioning and length of time in treatment variables influencing patients' therapeutic experience in group psychotherapy. International Journal of Group Psychotherapy, 33(4), 489–505.

Cartwright, D. (1968). The nature of group cohesiveness. In D. Cartwright, & A. Zander (Eds.), *Group Dynamics: Research and Theory* (pp 91–109). London: Tavistock Publications.

Colijn, S., Hoencamp, E., Snijders, H., Van der Spek, M., & Duivenvoorden, H. (1991). A comparison of curative factors in different types of group psychotherapy. *International Journal of Group Psychotherapy, 41*(3), 365–378.

Corey, G., Corey, M.S., & Callanan, P. (1990). Ethical issues in group work. *The Journal of Specialists in Group Work, 15*(2), 68–74.

Corey, M.S., & Corey, G. (1987). *Groups: Process and Practice.* Monterey, CA: Brooks/Cole Publishing Company.

Corsini, R. (1988). Adlerian groups. In S. Long (Ed.), *Six Group Therapies* (pp. 1–48). New York: Plenum Press.

Corsini, R. & Rosenberg, B. (1955). Mechanisms of group psychotherapy: Processes and dynamics. *Journal of Abnormal and Social Psychology, 51*, 406–411.

Couch, D.R., & Childers, J.H. (1987). Leadership strategies for instilling and maintaining hope in group counselling. *The Journal for Specialists in Group Work, 12*(4), 138–143.

Cullen, K., & Travin, S. (1990). Assessment and treatment of Spanish-speaking sex offenders: Special considerations. *Psychiatric Quarterly, 61*(4), 223–236.

Delgado, M. (1983). Hispanics and psychotherapeutic groups. *International Journal of Group Psychotherapy, 33*(4), 507–520.

Dies, R.R. (1974). Attitudes toward the training of group psychotherapists: Some interprofessional and experience-associated differences. *Small Group Behavior, 5*, 64–79.

Dies, R.R. (1983a). Bridging the gap between research and practice in group psychotherapy. In R.R. Dies & K.R. McKenzie, (Eds.), *Advances in Group Psychotherapy* (pp 1–26). New York: International Universities Press, Inc.

Dies, R.R. (1983b). Leadership in short-term groups. In R.R. Dies & K.R. MacKenzie, (Eds.), *Advances in Group Psychotherapy* (pp 27–78). New York: International Universities Press.

Dies, R.R. (1985). Research foundations for the future of group work. *Journal for the Specialists in Group Work, 10*(2), 68–73.

Dies, R.R., & Mackenzie, K.R. (1983). *Advances in Group Psychotherapy: Integrating Research and Practice*. New York: International Universities Press, Inc.

Dies, R.R., & Teleska, P.A. (1985). Negative outcome in group psychotherapy. In D.T. Mays & C.M. Franks (Eds.), *Negative Outcome in Psychotherapy and What to Do About It* (pp. 118–142). New York: Springer Publishing Company.

Dreikurs, R. (1957). Group psychotherapy from the point of view of Adlerian psychology. *International Journal of Group Psychotherapy, 7*, 363–365.

Drob, S., & Bernard, H.S. (1986). Time-limited group treatment of genital herpes patients. *International Journal of Group Psychotherapy, 36*(1), 133–144.

Droge, D., Arntson, P., & Norton, R. (1986). The social support function in epilepsy self-help groups. *Small Group Behaviour, 17*(2), 139–163.

Drum, D.J. (1990). Group therapy review. *The Counselling Psychologist, 18*(1), 131–138.

Duhatschek-Krause, A.L. (1989). A support group for patients and families facing life-threatening illness: Finding a solution to non-being. *Social Work with Groups, 12*(1), 55–67.

Farrelly, F., & Brandsma, J. (1974). *Provocative Therapy*. Cupertino, CA: Meta Publications Inc.

Finn, B., & Shakir, S.A. (1990). Intensive group psychotherapy of borderline patients. *Group, 4*(2), 99–110.

Frank, J.D., (1981). Therapeutic components shared by all psychotherapies. In J.H. Harvey & M.M. Parks (Eds.), *Psychotherapy, Research and Behaviour Change* (pp. 5–38) Washington, D.C: American Psychological Association.

Fry, W.F., & Salameh, W.A. (1987). *Handbook of Humor and Psychotherapy*. Sarasota, FL.: Professional Resources Exchange, Inc.

Fuhriman, A., & Burlingame, G. M. (1990). Consistency of matter: A comparative analysis of individual and group process variables. *Counselling Psychologist, 18*(1), 6–63.

Galenter, M. (1988). Zealous self-help groups as adjuncts to psychiatric treatment: A study of Recovery Inc. *American Journal of Psychiatry, 145*(10), 1248–1253.

Gartner, A., & Reissman, F. (1984). *The Self-Help Revolution*. New York: Human Science Press.

Gauron, E.F., & Rawlings, E.I. (1975). A procedure for orienting new members to group psychotherapy. *Small Group Behavior, 6*(3), 293–299.

Gill, S.J., & Barry, R.A. (1982). Group-focused counselling: Classifying the essential skills. *Personnel and Guidance Journal, 60*, 302–305.

Goldberg, F.S., McNeil, D.E., & Binder, R. L. (1988). Therapeutic factors in two forms of inpatient group psychotherapy: Music therapy and verbal therapy. *Group, 12*(3), 145–156.

Gregory, J. C., & McConnell, S. C. (1986). Ethical issues with psychotherapy in group contexts. *Psychotherapy in Private Practice, 4*(1), 51–62.

Harman, R.L. (1988). Gestalt group therapy. In S. Long (Ed.) *Six Group Therapies* (pp. 217–256). New York: Plenum Press.

Hartly, D., Roback, H.B., & Abramowitz, S.I. (1976). Deterioration effects in encounter groups. *American Psychologist, 31*, 247–255.

Hausman, M. (1979). Parents' group: How group members perceive curative factors. *Smith Studies in Social Work, 44*(3), 179–198.

Hobbs, M., Birtchnell, S., Harte, A., & Lacey, H. (1989). Therapeutic factors in short-term group therapy for women with bulimia. *International Journal of Eating Disorders, 8*(6), 623–633.

Horwitz, H. (1989). The evolution of a group-centered approach. In S. Tuttman, (ed.), *The Expanding World of Group Psychotherapy*. Madison, CT: International Universities Press.

Jacobs, M.K., & Goodman, M. (1989). Psychology and self-help groups: Predictions on a partnership. *American Psychologist, 44*(3), 536–545.

Jacobs, M., Jacobs, A., and Carior, N. (1973). Feedback II: the "credibility gap": delivery of positive and negative and emotional and behavioral feedback in groups. *Journal of Consulting and Clinical Psychology, 41*(2), 215–223.

Johnson, F. (1988). Encounter group therapy. In S. Long (Ed.), *Six Group Therapies* (pp: 115–158). New York: Plenum Press.

Joyce, A.S., Azim, H.F.A., & Morin, H. (1988). Brief crisis group psychotherapy versus the initial sessions of long-term group psychotherapy: An exploratory comparison. *Group, 12*(1), 3–17.

Kanas, N., & Barr, M.A. (1982). Outpatient alcoholics view group therapy. *Group, 6*(1), 17–20.

Kapur, R., Miller, K., & Mitchell, G. (1988). Therapeutic factors within inpatient and out-patient psychotherapy groups: Implications for therapeutic techniques. *British Journal of Psychiatry, 152*, 229–233.

Kaul, T.J., & Bednar, R.L. (1986). Experiential group research: Results, questions and suggestions. In S. Garfield & A. Bergin (Eds.), *Handbook of Psychotherapy and Behavior Change* (pp. 671–714). New York: Wiley.

Keith-Spiegel, P., & Koocher, G.P. (1985). *Ethics in Psychology Professional Standards and Cases*, New York: Random House.

Kellerman, P.F. (1985). Participant's perception of therapeutic factors in psychodrama. *Journal of Group Psychotherapy, Psychodrama and Sociometry, 38*(3), 123–132.

Kinzie, J., Leung, P., Bui, A., Ben, R., Keopraseuth, K.O., Riley, C., Fleck, J., & Ades, M. (1988). Group therapy with southeast Asian refugees. *Community Mental Health Journal, 24*(2), 157–167.

Kirshner, B.J., Dies, R.R., & Brown, R.A. (1978). Effects of experimental manipulation of self-disclosure on group cohesiveness. *Journal of Consulting and Clinical Psychology, 46*, 1171–1177.

Kivlighan, D.M. and Mullison, D. (1988). Participants' perception of therapeutic factors in group counseling: the role of interpersonal style and stage of group development. *Small Group Behavior, 19*(4) 452–468.

Kivlighan, D.M., Johnsen, B., & Fretz, B. (1987). Participant's perception of change mechanisms in career counseling groups: the role of emotional components in career problem solving. *Journal of Career Development, 14*(1), 35–44.

Klein, R.H. (1985). Some principles of short-term group therapy. *International Journal of Group Psychotherapy, 35*(3), 309–330.

Kline, W.B. (1990). Working with groups: responding to problem members. *The Journal for Specialists in Group Work, 15*(4), 195–200.

Koch, H.C., (1983). Changes in personal construing in three psychotherapy groups and a control group. *British Journal of Medical Psychology, 56*(3) 245–254.

Kotter, J.A. (1982). Ethics come of age. *Journal of Specialists in Group Work, 7*(3), 138–139.

Lakin, M. (1985). *The Helping Group: Therapeutic Principles and Issues.* Sydney: Addison-Wesley Publishing Company.

Lakin, M. (1986). Ethical challenges of group and dyadic psychotherapies: A comparative approach. *Professional Psychology: Research and Practice, 17*(9), 454–461.

Lakin, M. (1991). *Coping with Ethical Dilemmas in Psychotherapy.* New York: Pergamon Press.

Lambert, M.J., Shapiro, D.A., & Bergin, A.E., (1986). The effectiveness of psychotherapy. In S.L. Garfield & A.E. Bergin (Eds.), *Handbook of Psychotherapy and Behavior Change* (pp. 157–212). New York: Wiley.

LaTorre, R.A. (1977). Pretherapy role induction procedures. *Canadian Psychological Review, 18*, 308–321.

Latta, B. (1986). Applying the theory of reasoned action to group psychotherapy. *Journal of Group Psychotherapy, Psychodrama, and Sociometry, 39*(2). 58–65.

Leahey, M., & Wallace, E. (1988). Strategic groups: One perspective on integrating strategic and group therapies. *The Journal for Specialists in Group Work, 13*(4), 209–217.

Lesowitz, M., Kalter, N., Pickar, J., Chethik, M., & Schaefer, M. (1987). School-based developmental facilitation groups for children of divorce: Issues of group process. *Psychotherapy, 24*, 90–95.

Lesca, M., Yalom, .R. & Norden, M. (1985). The value of inpatient group psychotherapy: Patients' perceptions. *International Journal of Group Psychotherapy, 35*(3), 411–433.

Levitt, D.B. (1986). Group support in the treatment of PMS. *Journal of Psychosocial Nursing & Mental Health Services, 24*(1), 23–27.

Lewis, P. (1987). Therapeutic change in groups: An interactional perspective. *Small Group Behavior, 18*(4), 548–556.

Llewelyn, S.P., & Haslett, A.V.J. (1986). Factors perceived as helpful by the members of self-help groups: An exploratory study. *British Journal of Guidance and Counselling, 14*(3), 252–262.

Lichtenberg, J.W., & Knox, P.L. (1991). Order out of chaos: a structural analysis of group therapy, *Journal of Counselling Psychology, 38*(3), 279–288.

Lieberman, M. (1983). Comparative analysis of change mechanisms in groups. In R.R. Dies & K.R. MacKenzie (Eds.) *Advances in group psychotherapy: integrating research and practice* (pp. 191–208). New York: International Universities Press.

Lieberman, M.A. (1990). Understanding how groups work: A study of homogeneous peer group failures. *International Journal of Group Psychotherapy, 40*(1), 31–52.

Lieberman, M., & Gourash-Bliwise, N. (1982). *Comparisons among peer and professionally directed groups for the elderly: Implications for the development of self-help groups.* Unpublished manuscript, University of Chicago, Chicago.

Lieberman, M., Yalom, I. & Miles, M. (1973). *Encounter Groups First Facts.* New York: Basic Books, Inc.

Long, S. (1988). *Six Group Therapies.* New York: Plenum Press.

McCallum, M., & Piper, W.E. (1990). A controlled study of effectiveness and patient suitability for short-term group psychotherapy. *International Journal of Group Psychotherapy, 40*(4), 431–452.

MacDevitt, J.W., & Sanislow, C. (1987). Curative factors in offenders' groups. *Small Group Behavior, 18*(1), 72–81.

Mackenzie, K.R. (1983). The clinical application of a group climate measure. In R.R.Dies & K.R. Mackenzie (Eds.), *Advances in Group Psychotherapy: Integrating Research and Practice* (pp. 159–170). New York: International Universities Press.

Mackenzie, K.R., Dies, R.R., Cohche, E., Rutan, J.S., & Stone, W.N. (1987). An analysis of AGPA Institute groups. *International Journal of Group Psychotherapy, 37*(1), 55–74.

MacKenzie, K.R., & Livesley, W.J. (1983). A developmental model for brief group therapy. In R.R. Dies & K.R. MacKenzie (Eds.), *Advances in Group Psychotherapy: Integrating Research and Practice* (pp. 101–116). New York: International Universities Press.

Mackie-Ramos, R.L., & Rice, J.M. (1988). Group psychotherapy with methadone-maintained pregnant women. *Journal of Substance Abuse Treatment, 5,* 151–161.

Marcovitz, R.J. & Smith, J.E. (1983). Patients' perceptions of curative factors in short-term group psychotherapy. *International Journal of Group Psychotherapy, 33*(1), 21–39.

Moreno, J.L. (1970). The Viennese origins of the encounter movement, paving the way for existentialism, group psychotherapy, and psychodrama. *Group Psychotherapy, 22,* 7–16.

Munich & Astrachan.B. (1983). Group Dynamics. In H.I. Kaplan and B.J. Sadock (Eds.), *Comprehensive Group Psychotherapy* London: Williams & Wilkins.

Murphy, J.F., & Cannon, D.J. (1986). Avoiding early dropouts: Patient selection and preparation techniques. *Journal of Psychosocial Nursing and Mental Health Services, 24*(9), 21–26.

Naar, R. (1982). *A Primer of Group Psychotherapy.* New York: Human Sciences Press, Inc.

Napier, R.W., & Gershenfeld, M.K., (1981). *Groups* (2nd ed.). Boston: Houghton Mifflin Company.

Ohlsen, M. (1977). *Group Counselling* (2nd ed). Sydney: Holt, Rinehart & Winston.

Parker, R.S. (1972). Can group therapy be harmful to the individual? *Journal of Clinical Issues in Psychology, 3*(2), 22–24.

Parson, E.R. (1985). Post-traumatic accelerated cohesion: its recognition and management in group treatment of Vietnam veterans. *Group, 9*(4), 10–23.

Perls, F.S. (1969). *In and Out the Garbage Pail.* Toronto: Bantam Books.

Phipps, L.B., & Zastowny, T.R. (1988). Leadership behavior, group climate and outcome in group psychotherapy: A study of outpatient psychotherapy groups. *Group, 12*(3), 157–171.

Pietz, C.A., & Mann, J.P. (1989). Importance of having a female cotherapist in a child molesters' group. *Professional Psychology: Research and Practice, 20*(4), 265–268.

Piper, W.E. (1991). Brief group psychotherapy. *Psychiatric Annals, 21*(7), 419–423.

Piper, W.E., & Perrault, E.L. (1989). Pretherapy preparation for group members. *International Journal of Group Psychotherapy, 39*(1), 17–34.

Poey, K. (1985). Guidelines for the practice of brief, dynamic, group therapy. *International Journal of Group Psychotherapy, 35*(3), 331–353.

Polcin, D.L. (1991). Working with groups: prescriptive group leadership. *The Journal for Specialists in Group Work, 16*(1) 8–15.

Power, M.J. (1985). The selection of patients for group therapy. *International Journal of Social Psychiatry, 31*(4), 290–297.

Richards, R.L., Burlingame, G.M., & Fuhriman, A. (1990). Theme-oriented group therapy. *The Counselling Psychologist, 18*(1), 80–92.

Rinehart, L. (1971). *The Dice Man.* London: Grafton Books.

Roark, A.E., & Sharah, H.S. (1989). Factors related to group cohesiveness. *Small Group Behavior, 20*(1), 62–69.

Robinson-Smith, N. (1985). Bulimia and student counselling. *British Journal of Guidance and Counselling, 13*(2), 147–156.

Rogers, C. (1970). *Carl Rogers on Encounter Groups.* New York: Harper & Row.

Rowe, W. and Winborn, B. (1973). What people fear about group work: an analysis of 36 selected critical articles. *Educational Technology, 13*(1), 53–57.

Sadock, B.J., & Kaplan, H.I. (1983). History of group psychotherapy. In H.I. Kaplan & B.J. Sadock, (Eds.), *Comprehensive Group Psychotherapy.* London: Williams & Wilkins.

Schaefer, C., Coyne, J.C. & Lazarus, R.S. (1981). The health-related functions of social support. *Journal of Behavioral Medicine, 4*, 381–406.

Scheidlinger, S. (1984). Group psychotherapy in the 1980s: Problems and prospects. *American Journal of Psychotherapy, 38*(4), 494–504.

Schutz, W. (1978). *FIRO Awareness Manual*. Palo Alto, California: Consulting Psychologists Press.

Schutz, W.C. (1967). *Joy: Expanding Human Awareness*. New York: Grove Press, Inc.

Shaffer, J., & Galinsky, M. (1974). *Models of Group Therapy and Sensitivity Training*. Englewood Cliffs, New Jersey: Prentice-Hall.

Shapiro, J.L. (1978). *Methods of Group Psychotherapy and Encounter: A Tradition of Innovation*. Ithaca, N.Y.: F.E. Peacock Publishers, Inc.

Silverman, P. R. (1986). The perils of borrowing: Roles of the professional in mutual help groups. *Journal for Specialists in Group Work, 11*(2), 68–73.

Smith, K.K., & Berg, D.N. (1987). A paradoxical conception of group dynamics. *Human Relations, 40*(10), 633–658.

Smith, P. (1980). *Small Groups and Personal Change*. London: Methuen & Co.

Stern, M., Plionis, E., & Kaslow, L. (1984). Group process expectations and outcome with post-myocardial infarction patients. *General Hospital Psychiatry, 6*, 101–108.

Stevens, E., & Salisbury, J. (1984). Group therapy for bulimic adults. *American Journal of Orthopsychiatry, 54*(1), 156–161.

Stockton, R., & Morran, D. (1982). Reviews and perspectives of critical dimensions in therapeutic small group research. In G.M. Gazda, (Ed.). *Basic Approaches to Group Psychotherapy and Group Counselling* (pp: 37–85). Springfield, Ill: Thomas.

Taylor, S.E., Falke, R.L., Shoptaw, S.J., & Lichtman, R.R. (1986). Social support, support groups, and the cancer patient. *Journal of Consulting and Clinical Psychology, 54*(5), 608–615.

Thayer, V. (1986). The use of a support group for borderline mothers of adolescents. *Social Work with Groups, 9*(2), 57–71.

The Australian Psychological Society, (1986). *Code of Professional Conduct*.

Tillitski, C.J. (1990). A meta-analysis of estimated effect sizes for group versus individual versus control treatments. *International Journal of Group Psychotherapy, 40*(2), 215–224.

Toseland, R.W. & Siporin, M. (1986). When to recommend group treatment: A review of the clinical and research literature. *International Journal of Group Psychotherapy, 36*, 171–201.

Tsui, P., & Schultz, G.L. (1988). Ethic factors in group process: Cultural dynamics in multi-ethnic therapy groups. *American Journal of Orthopsychiatry, 58*(1), 136–142.

Tuckman, B.W. (1965). Developmental sequence in small groups. *Psychological Bulletin, 63*, 394–399.

Tuttman, S. (1989). *The Expanding World of Group Psychotherapy*. Madison, CT: International Universities Press.

Tuttman, S. (1991). On utilizing humor in group psychotherapy. *Group, 15*(4), 246–256.

Unger, R. (1989). Selection and composition criteria in group psychotherapy. *Journal for Specialists in Group Work, 14*(3), 151–157.

Waldo, M. (1985). A curative factor framework for conceptualizing group counseling. *Journal of Counseling and Development, 64*, 52–64.

Waltman, D.E. & Zimpfer, D.G. (1988). Composition, structure, and duration of treatment. *Small Group Behavior, 19*(2), 171–184.

Weiner, M. F. (1983a). The assessment and resolution of impasse in group psychotherapy. *International Journal of Group Psychotherapy, 33*(3), 313–331.

Weiner, M.F. (1983b). The role of the leader in group psychotherapy. In H.I. Kaplan & B.J. Sadock (Eds.), *Comprehensive Group Psychotherapy* (pp: 54–63). London: Williams & Wilkins.

Whalen, G.S., & Mushet, G.L. (1986). Consumers' views of the helpful aspects of an in-patient psychotherapy group: A preliminary communication. *British Journal of Medical Psychology, 59*, 337–339.

Whitaker, D. (1985). *Using Groups to Help People*. London: Routledge and Kegan Paul.

Wilson, R.F., Conyne, R.K., Bardgett, D.A., & Smith-Hartle, A. (1987). Marketing of group counseling services. *Journal for Specialists in Group Work, 12*(1), 10–17.

Yalom, I. (1970). *The Theory and Practice of Group Psychotherapy*. New York: Basic Books, Inc.

Yalom, I. (1975). *The Theory and Practice of Group Psychotherapy* (2nd ed.). New York: Basic Books, Inc.

Yalom, I. (1983). *Inpatient Group Psychotherapy*. New York: Basic Books, Inc.

Yalom, I. (1985) *The Theory and Practice of Group Psychotherapy* (3rd ed.). New York: Basic Books, Inc.

Zimpfer, D. (1986). Planning for groups based on their developmental phases. *Journal for Specialists in Group Work, 11*(3), 180–187.

AUTHOR INDEX

SUBJECT INDEX